LIMPENHOE SOUTHWOOD
CANTLEY

VILLAGE SIGNS in NORFOLK

BOOK 2

100 Photographs by Frances Procter

100 Sketches by Philippa Miller

BLACK HORSE BOOKS

NORWICH

July 1979

Dear Readers,

This is our second book about the stories, legends and facts portrayed on the Village and Town signs in Norfolk. The Jubilee of our Queen, and that of the Women's Institutes, more or less coinciding, gave great incentive to the people of Norfolk to have social events in their villages, in order to raise funds and acquire a sign of their own.

As we said in our first book, King Edward VII and his son King George V suggested and encouraged the idea of having signs to begin with, and at least three bear the date 1912 upon them still!

We describe here 100 more signs with photographs, sketches, maps and index, and as things are going at present we foresee that a third book will become essential.

This growing popularity for erecting distinctive and original signs, necessitating much delving into the past, has engendered a new Folk Art of which Norfolk may very well be proud, and which is rapidly spreading to other counties. Its greatest merit lies in the fact that the research, planning and execution encourages and fosters a community spirit within the village, in an age when so much is in danger of resulting in impersonal standardization and dull uniformity.

Our county is one of the largest in England extending from Wisbech to Yarmouth, and Blakeney to Scole. To discover all the signs, and the legends, requires much travelling and many enquiries, hence we have included, on the cover of our book, signs from the north, south, east and west, so that our county, we hope, is well represented.

Mr. Carter still carries out a great many village signs, but also, we are happy to note, more and more local talent is being sought, and brought to light, within the communities.

There has also grown up the hobby of sign-hunting. Many people have told us how much they enjoy searching out and photographing the signs, with our book as guide, when on holiday in Norfolk; in fact some come especially for that purpose.

We, as lovers of all Norfolk things, take pleasure in the fact that after 67 years all our village signs still proudly stand, adding distinction and giving character to their locality.

Frances Procter

Philippa Miller

ACLE

Acle is a small market town with a fine church, a station, and with a meeting of the ways around a tiny green on which stands the Village Sign and the Folly tree, a fine old elm which has survived for more than 100 years.

Two roads lead to Norwich and two to Yarmouth, the newer one (1833) in a straight line across the marshes for about nine miles. The older one leads to Acle Bridge, a well-known and popular boating centre when exploring the Norfolk Broads.

Acle's Thursday market draws people from miles around. The very attractive Sign was put up in the summer of 1974 and was given by Mr. N. Chalk, and the base by Mr. Hay, both Acle businessmen. It is double-sided and was carved by Mr. Harry Carter of Swaffham.

The sign shows the old three-arched bridge over the Bure and also Acle Church. A windmill too can be seen in the distance, on one side a wagon and horses are being driven up to the bridge, whereas if you go over and look at the other side of the bridge, so to speak, you will see that a wherry is sailing down the river.

On the shore is the "Folly" tree which still exists. It is a little uncertain as to how it got its name, the local people proffer various ideas. Below the name is a shield with the device indicating St. Edmund, the patron saint of the church.

ACLE – THE FOLLY TREE

ACLE

ACLE

ALDBOROUGH

Aldborough has a large and attractive green around which the village is built, and on the southern corner has been placed the Village Sign, which recently, we noticed, has been provided with a tiny roof of thatch.

The two sides recall different aspects of village life; one shows the tanning industry of the past. In Kelly's Directory of 1888 and White's of 1845 can be found the names of tanner, currier, saddler and fellmonger, all concerned with the production of leather and leather goods.

The other side of the Sign displays all the gaiety of a village fair, which is still one of the highlights of the year, though not perhaps quite in the same form. In the past famous stock fairs were held every year in midsummer, for two whole days, and have provided the opportunity for great annual festivities for over 700 years.

Aldborough's Sign was designed and made by Mr. Harry Carter and presented to the Parish Council by Aldborough and Thurgarton Women's Institute in 1975.

Another thing, so nostalgic of our country's rural past, is that here, on many a day in summer one is greeted by the sight of a friendly game of cricket in progress, and all the players in white flannels too! — the epitome of sunny care-free days in the best and most English tradition.

ALDBOROUGH

ALDBOROUGH

ANTINGHAM

The setting of Antingham Village Sign is a quiet, triangular green, flanked on one side by the road from North Walsham to Cromer, and where rough grasses and low rushes grow round the edges of a small pond. In the background may be seen two churches in one enclosure; one is the ruined church of St. Margaret, and the other is the parish church of St. Mary. It is a typical scene of peaceful East Anglia.

This sign is pleasing and well proportioned, and made in polished natural oak, thus giving a warm, glowing effect, and is both dignified and satisfying to the eye. It is shaped like a cross, the crossbar bearing the name Antingham incised in bold lettering; above it stands a shield carved with the Suffield family coat of arms. On either side are two panels mounted on ironwork brackets. The one on the right shows the two churches already mentioned, the other shows two wherries — such as would have been seen on the now ruined North Walsham canal along which they sailed here bearing cargoes of various commodities, and taking away bone manure from the mills at Antingham — a valuable trade before the days of modern fertilizers.

This sign is entirely of local origin: designed by a parishioner, it was carved by Mr. Terry Read, and the wrought iron-work was carried out by Mr. John Todrayner. The handsome base was built voluntarily by two more parishioners.

The sign was unveiled by the Hon. Doris Harbord — herself a descendant of the Suffield family. The cost of the sign was borne by the parishioners and the Village Hall Committee.

ANTINGHAM

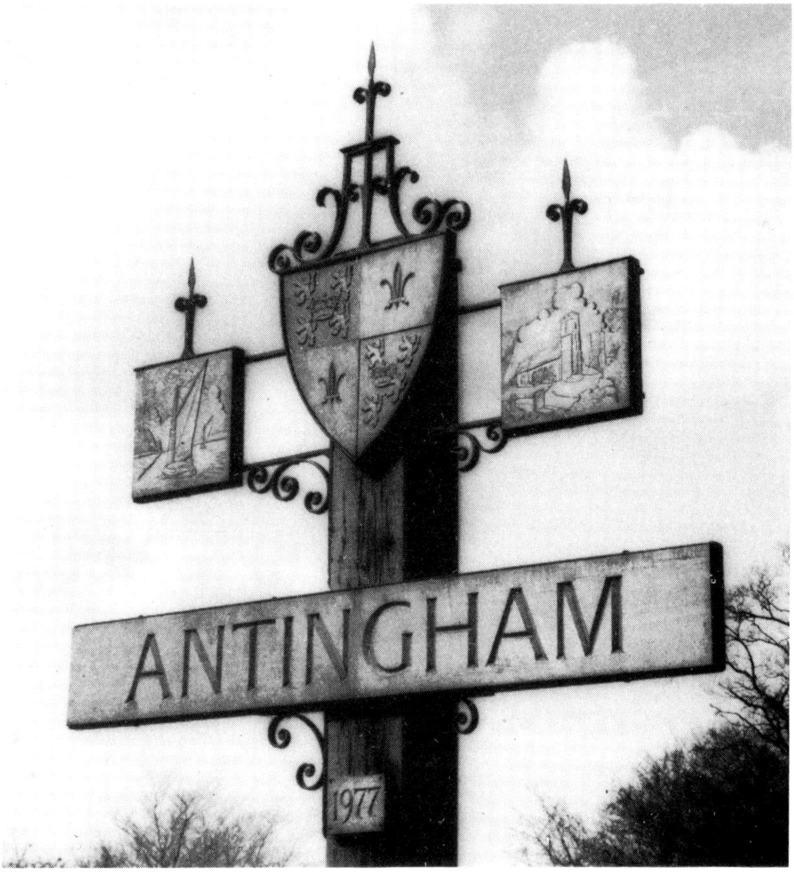
ANTINGHAM
1977

ATTLEBOROUGH

Attleborough is a busy market town on the main road from Norwich to London and the Sign stands among the trees on the central Green, which, due to the one-way system, has to be approached from the Thetford side. Mr. Harry Carter of Swaffham carved and painted the double-sided Sign, and it is typical of the T shape we find in most town Signs. It was put up in 1975. Above the name is the device adopted by the town, incorporating a lion, mitre, plough and sheaf of corn.

The pictures below are both concerned with cider-making, which was for centuries centred on this part of Norfolk. Banham Manor, originally the home of the Gaymer family, is but a few miles away. Here cider was made for many years before the factory was moved to Attleborough in 1896.

The two scenes on the Sign are taken from illustrations in an old publication — John Worlidge's "Vinetum Brittanicum" of 1676; one shows the apple mill with a man turning the wheel to operate the grinder, and the other shows a simple screw press, with the lever being pulled to press the pulp received from the mill. Both illustrations thus deal only with the extraction of juice, which will then be fermented in casks.

Dessert, cooking and cider apples from Norfolk normally supply the Gaymer business with enough for their purposes. They are grown too in recent years by the firm. This apple wine takes up to two years to make, and twenty-eight million gallons were produced in one year.

Below the panels are shields wich show two old-fashioned besoms, (brooms are still made in the district) and on each side is a turkey, reminding us of yet another industry carried on in the vicinity.

Turkeys were brought to England in the 16th century, they were natives of North America. In the days before easy transport turkeys were walked to the London markets! Tough birds? The old-time Michaelmas Turkey Fair was restarted in December 1974.

Some of the funds towards the cost of the Sign were raised by the efforts of several Norfolk antique dealers who arranged a sale especially for that purpose, and the money was duly handed to the treasurer of the Chamber of Trade.

BACTON

Thinking of Bacton one is reminded of the old Italian deity — Jason, from whose name is derived the month of January, and who is always represented as having a head to the front and one to the back, so that he could see both backwards and forwards — as the month of January looks back to the old year and forwards to the new. At Bacton the backwards glance is to look at what has been described as one of the prettiest villages in this part of Norfolk, and to see nearby a reminder of the great past in the remains of its famous old C12 priory of Bromholm with its relic of the True Cross, which was reputed to perform miracles, and even to restore the dead to life! Countless pilgrims visited the priory from near and far, and it became famous and rich through their generous gifts to it. Little remains now of its magnificence but part of its old gateway, a farmhouse, and fragments of wall.

The forwards look is to the extensive buildings, pylons, and gasometers, with other components of the North Sea gas installation — incidentally the first in Britain — that take up so much space in Bacton.

True, every effort has been made to prevent it from becoming too much of an eyesore by landscaping the surroundings, but it has badly scarred the face that looks towards the future, for such is the sacrifice exacted to pay the price for progress and economic security.

But the backward looking glance sees that a beautiful village sign has enhanced and added to the oldest and most picturesque part. It was made by Mr. Harry Carter on the same lines as the one at Edingthorpe, only two miles away. It shows in a large central panel, a monk from the Cluniac priory, clothed in the black habit of a Benedictine, whilst the smaller panels show the fishing and farming occupations of Bacton.

BACTON

The base is large and impressive, and sets off the sign very well. It was erected to commemorate the Queen's Silver Jubilee. **Funds** were raised by a donation from the Parish Council and much effort from **the** village to augment it. Keswick is a hamlet on the cliffs nearby, almost entirely given over to caravans and holiday bungalows.

BANHAM

Banham is as picturesque a village as you could wish to see, and accordingly it is very photogenic. Here one sees a rectangular green flanked on two sides by magnificent lime trees, and old houses showing thatch and overhanging storeys, and Dutch gables. Behind it is a fine medieval church with a beautiful porch. Those interested in both church and domestic architecture will find much to interest them.

Various aspects of the village will delight the eye, and it is a happy experience to see the shadows of the waving branches of the lime trees flickering on the walls of the colour washed houses; or in the spring to see the exquisitely delicate green leaves shimmering against a blue sky.

The village sign has been erected at one end of the green, and it was made by residents of the village, using Banham oak and stones, which adds to the attractions of their sign, of which they must surely feel very proud. It shows a kiln, obviously functioning, whilst beside it is an apple tree, and under it a man pressing apples. This pleasing little scene refers to the fact that at one time, about three quarters of a mile west of the village, were factories at which tiles, bricks and chimneypots were made; thanks to the excellent clay to be found there, which so admirably suited the purpose. Also Banham was the centre of a cider making industry which was owned by Gaymer and Son, already — even in those days — an old established firm.

BANHAM

A sense of fun seems to bubble up in this sign, because on the reverse side is seen a man eating an apple, and a cat, an owl and a mouse have appeared. One cannot help wondering if the owl has predatory designs on the mouse, and if the cat is not entertaining similar thoughts regarding the owl?

This delightful sign was provided for by the Silver Jubilee funds collected by the residents. It was constructed by Mr. Steve Egleton, and the base was built by Mr. Len Birch.

BAWBURGH

Norfolk is a very large county, but even so it is surprising to learn that it has seven hundred villages in it. But of all these it is most exceptionable to be able to lay claim to being the burial place of a saint whose fame spread far and wide. Bawburgh, picturesque and unspoilt, stands on the upper reaches of the river Yare, and close to the triple-arched bridge which crosses it, is to be seen a delightful old watermill. Recently yet another point of interest has been added to it, and that is a truly beautiful village sign, which stands on a small patch of green on the way to the church. This lovely carved oak sign naturally depicts the saint — St. Walstan; Taverham, a village about four miles away, also shows St. Walstan on their sign, for he lived there all his working days. He was an early Christian mystic, preceding St. Francis of Assisi by 200 years, and Mother Julian of Norwich by 350 years, so it cannot be said that he derived anything from them! There was very little book-learning then, for very few people were able to write, and teaching would be largely traditional, but so deeply touched were the hearts of those who revered him, that his memory is retained even to this day. He was a humble and devout man, preferring to live a simple working life amongst the farmers and peasants. He was the son of a Saxon king and his mother was St. Blida, and he was born in Suffolk: but he gave up his rank and wealth to live a life of devotion and humility amongst the poor and unlearned peasants, where he worked as a farm labourer. When he was dying they asked him where he wished to be buried, and he directed that his body should be placed on a farm wagon, which was to be drawn by two yoked oxen, and that wherever they took him and then stopped, there they should bury him. The oxen wended their way to Costessey, where they rested awhile, and after they proceeded on their way it was seen that where his body had rested a spring of water appeared. They reached Bawburgh where the oxen finally stopped. They dug his grave on the north side of the church, and later a shrine was built over it. Also another spring gushed up, and it became known for its healing properties; it was

WATERMILL, BAWBURGH

called St. Walstan's Well, and pilgrimages were made to it for healing over the centuries. The last one took place as recently as 1912. St. Walstan is sometimes depicted in Norfolk churches where he carries a sceptre and a scythe, symbolical of his royal birth and his life as a labourer. In Bawburgh village sign you will see a carved representation of him with arms outstretched to two little lambs, to show his love for nature, and his compassion for all small and defenceless creatures. In the background are to be seen the church and the two oxen.

On the back of the sign is incised "Elizabeth II, and the artists's monogram — A. W. entwined. This beautifully rendered sign was carved by a Yorkshire artist, Mr. Alex Whammond, who must be congratulated on his exquisite and sensitive carving, which is truly inspired, and will give pleasure and satisfaction to all who see it, and especially those who remember the saint with affection.

The people of Bawburgh must feel very proud of this sign which they have had erected.

BEESTON
(formerly known as Beeston next Mileham)

Recently, in a conversation about village signs, a friend said, "I think that a village sign gives dignity to a village", which when you come to think of it, is a very true observation to make. And when Mr. Ian Wallace, the well known singer, unveiled the sign at West Runton, where he now lives, he said, "Village signs are an expression of pride on the part of the village, and an expression of welcome to the visitors". Indeed, one feels in a village that lacks one, there is certainly something missing that is desirable, in order to give it completion.

Beeston is a village that is somewhat scattered, which is not uncommon in a farming community, where, of necessity, farmhouses must lie within the confines of their own fields. Even the church is three quarters of a mile away; although there are traces of the remains of buildings next to it, which shows that it was not always remote from habitations. Beeston has no pretensions to a historic past, nor distinctions of any kind; its past lies buried in its fields, which have been cultivated for untold centuries.

In the centre of its sign is a striking coat of arms, those of the Lord of the Manor of Beeston who was the Earl of Arundel and Mileham, which is two miles away, where there are remains of a ruined castle, of which little is known, but with which it is very likely that the past inhabitants of Beeston were much concerned. In the left hand spandrel of the sign one sees an arrowhead similar to the one carved on the church wall in 1695, which is symbolical of a ploughshare, the due paid to the Lord of the Manor when a bondsman took over a strip of land at Beeston.

CHURCH - BEESTON N^R MILEHAM

From the right hand spandrel one can see that this is a Jubilee sign. It was made by Mr. Harry Carter, and mounted on a fine plinth of brick and flint. The cost was borne by the Jubilee Committee who presented to the village this handsome sign, commemorating its fine, agricultural past, by showing not only the plough share but the plough itself on the top part of the sign.

BELTON

Going around Norfolk, one cannot fail to notice how almost every village has undergone a change, and how modern houses and bungalows have sprung up everywhere. Sometimes one deplores it, but with so many people wanting to move out of the towns it is inevitable. Then, too, many people have visited Norfolk on holiday, have fallen in love with it, and have determined to retire here. Small wonder, for it is a friendly, peaceful county, with pure air, fine views, and magnificent rolling skies. So, the villages expand; but in time, when the new buildings have become weathered and mellowed, and the hedgeless, open gardens lend colour and beauty to the eye, it all becomes harmonious and acceptable, and one no longer resents the change. Just such a place is Belton; and it is there, in the middle of a housing estate that one finds the village sign. It shows in glowing colours a figure standing in a typical country scene; whilst in the spandrels below are painted fruit and flowers grown locally.

The sign was erected to the memory of the late Mr. John Berry, a former parish and borough councillor, who had thought of the idea of a village sign, and had paid for it, but had, unfortunately died before its completion. He had wanted to show his appreciation to Belton, because, he had said, "Belton has always been very good to me, and I would like to do something in return."

The sign depicts John Ives, who was born in 1788 (or 9), and died in Belton at the early age of 24½ years. The shield shows the coat of arms of the Ives family, a gold chevron between three Moor's heads. His tomb can be seen in the church.

Despite his age he became one of East Anglia's most promising young antiquaries. His father and grandfather were wealthy merchants, who lived in Yarmouth and owned extensive properties in Belton and the Lothingland countryside. At that time Belton was in Suffolk, but since the altering of county boundaries Belton now lies in Norfolk.

BELTON —
NEAR THE KINGS HEAD

Recently a booklet has been published by Mr. Norman Scarfe entitled "John Ives, F.R.S., F.S.A. Suffolk Herald Extraordinary 1751-1756." It should make interesting reading about this brilliant and unusual young man. The sign was made by Mr. Harry Carter of Swaffham.

BODHAM

Bodham is another village set in the midst of agricultural country, with enough modern houses and bungalows to make you realise that it has grown of recent years, as so many of our Norfolk villages have; but it has not brought to your notice that farming is the main occupation here; instead it has struck an entirely new theme, for it shows a representation of a medieval tax collector about his employment. This man's name — Boda — is mentioned in Domesday Book, which confirms his existence, and also the fact that he lived here. Now the usual assumption is that a tax collector collects money, and here on this sign we see the bags in which the cash was put; but from the picture we may conclude that if money was not forthcoming (and in those days barter and exchange was a common way of trading in a small way) then, in the paying of taxes by those without coin of the realm, any portable goods applicable to a man's trade would be acceptable; hence, one may suppose, *that* is the reason for the livestock: which must have made a tax collector's profession more than a little difficult at times!

A few years ago there was a letter, in the Eastern Daily Press, to the editor from a disgruntled person, who must have harboured a grudge about village signs, dismissing them from further consideration, and peevishly complaining that "they all looked alike"! (The person protesting didn't seem to realise that there was no obligation to look if he preferred not to!) Remembering all those signs that have been erected up to the present — more than 250 at the time of writing — is it not remarkable that so much variety has been shown, and with so much ingenuity?

BODHAM

Congratulations should be given to this village for thinking of yet another theme to add interest to the much admired village signs, by researching so thoroughly into their recorded past, and bringing more knowledge to us of the everyday life of the common people in days gone by.

This sign was the gift of the Bodham and District Women's Institute to mark the occasion of the Queen's Silver Jubilee. The sign was made by Mr. Harry Carter, who has made so many of our village signs in Norfolk.

BRADWELL

Until fairly recently when the county boundaries were altered Bradwell was in Suffolk, but now it is included within the boundary of Norfolk. Not so long ago it was a tiny village — but nowadays it is very large, owing to the housing estates which have grown around it, and have infused new life into a village which might so easily have dwindled — like many another — instead of which, with young and growing families, it can now have a future as well as a past!

Another thing it has gained, and that is a very fine sign. One cannot see it without thinking how attractive it is with the figure of St. Nicholas looking down so benignly, and the golden rayed sun rising behind him. And benign St. Nicholas certainly was, and without doubt the most genial and best loved saint in the whole Calendar. You, yourself, in your childhood days had great faith in him, even to the extent possibly of writing a letter to him, hoping that at Christmas he would come down your chimney and fill your stocking with presents! On the continent children think of him as "good St. Nicholas", but their custom is to leave their shoes by the fireplace instead. The name Santa Claus comes via America — from the Dutch dialect form of his name.

In art saints always have their own emblems by which they are recognised. St. Nicholas of Myra is usually shown with three bags of gold, and he is sometimes connected with Bari, because his relics were stolen from Myra and taken to Bari! The three bags of gold illustrate his kindly concern, for when he heard of three young women who would have been reduced to a life of shame, because their father was too poor to provide them with dowries, he threw into their window, at night, three bags of gold to enable them to marry honourably. This emblem can be seen on the very small panel below the large one.

BRADWELL

The other symbols on the sign include a man ploughing, which indicates that agriculture is still the main occupation here, whilst the mill is to remind us of the old mill which once ground corn. Finally the sun, which appears in this land on the eastern coast of Norfolk, earlier than in any other part of England, is to recall the earliest recorded building in Bradwell — the Rising Sun Inn.

BRESSINGHAM

Bressingham is near the southern border of Norfolk and is well known, for it has achieved fame from the successful ventures of Mr. Alan Bloom, who has devoted his time to creating beautiful gardens and collecting and exhibiting famous engines from the days of steam. Such attractions are the delight of thousands of visitors each summer.

Bressingham Gardens and the church lie to the south of the main road from Diss, but the village houses are to be found along a minor road leading north towards Boyland, and here, where the road forks, is the Village Sign.

Bressingham and Roydon Women's Institute made great efforts, everyone helping in dozens of ways to produce enough money to be able to give a sign to each village, in order to celebrate their Jubilee in 1974.

Mr. Harry Carter designed the signs, and in studying the village histories, discovered the existence, long ago, of a judge, Sir Richard Boyland, who, it appears, was guilty of "manifest corruption" and was fined 4000 marks by King Edward I!

However, Sir Richard retired discreetly to the Bressingham area and was able to find enough funds to build the church there in 1280. Boyland Hall, complete with moat was situated a mile or so north of the church and possessed a remarkable vault or conduit, and a water supply that never freezes.

On the Sign we see depicted both Sir Richard Boyland and his church among the trees. The present church was rebuilt in 1527.

BRESSINGHAM GARDENS

BRESSINGHAM

BRISTON

Briston is a large, scattered village, set in pretty, pastoral country. It is only one mile from Melton Constable, a place which grew in importance and size, in the heydey of the railway era. It might seem to a stranger that Briston owes its existence to Melton Constable, as a kind of overspill village, but it has a history of such antiquity that its name is in Domesday Book, where it is called Burstuna. Its new village sign will tell you much that is of interest. It is erected at the northern end of the village, on a tiny patch of grass where the road diverges; and it is worth noticing that the donors have placed over it a small, slender canopy to give it some protection from weathering etc., which it does without casting shadows on it. The Sign is delicately coloured, and attractive to look at. It takes the form of a shield, and below the name which is placed across the top, is a large red St. George's cross, and in each quarter are symbols which are very significant. The five crowns represent the five manors which lie within the parish boundaries. The heads of a pig, a sheep, and a cow, with a gate above them, stand for the Tuesday Market which was held each week. The sheaves of corn inform us that agriculture was carried on throughout the ages. The wavy blue lines indicate that one of the sources of the river Bure rises in the village. In the centre can be seen a merry-go-round, and it tells that a twice yearly fair was held here, and still continues.

In the past fairs were very important events. They could only be held by royal charter, and were only held to promote trades. It gave an opportunity for simple amusements to take place, but only as sideshows to the main business in hand. Fairs, such as we know them are travelling "amusement parks", and bear no comparison to the ancient fairs, which had a serious intent, and so were necessary for the development of commercial enterprises. This sign is double sided, and on each side is a small panel with "E.R. II" carved on it, to indicate, of course, that this is a Silver Jubilee sign.

BRISTON

Mr. K. F. Ashwell, the Chairman of the Parish Council was responsible for organising the arrangement for the making and erection of the sign, which was designed by a local artist Mr. Mike Bignold, and was made by Mr. Harry Carter. It was paid for by contributions from individuals and various organisations in the village. The base was made by Parish Council members who also erected the sign.

It contrives to enhance and add dignity to this ancient village which was clearly an important place in medieval and later times.

BRUNDALL

Brundall, united with Bradeston, is a long village and has grown up along a high ridge above a loop in the river Yare. It is pleasantly wooded with some fine trees and houses, and recently there has been an extensive development and change. But the Village Sign, erected in 1975, recalls an older epoch of the main industry of today — that of boat-building beside the river below the village. The very successful modern firms here design and build luxury motor cruisers and are busy with the letting of holiday boats of all kinds.

The building and repairing of boats both large and small has obviously been carried on for many years, probably since the Broads were opened up during the latter half of the 19th century, and also much earlier, as far back as the Viking invasions, for the high ridge at Brundall would have provided safe landfall in the days when the great tidal estuaries penetrated far inland. The Romans are said to have had a dockyard here for repairs to their galleys (some traces of a Roman villa and fragments of pottery have been found). Thus on the painted metal Sign we see a partly completed galley and others moored nearby.

The Sign was given by the Women's Institute to commemorate their Diamond Jubilee, and stands near the centre of the village.

BRUNDALL

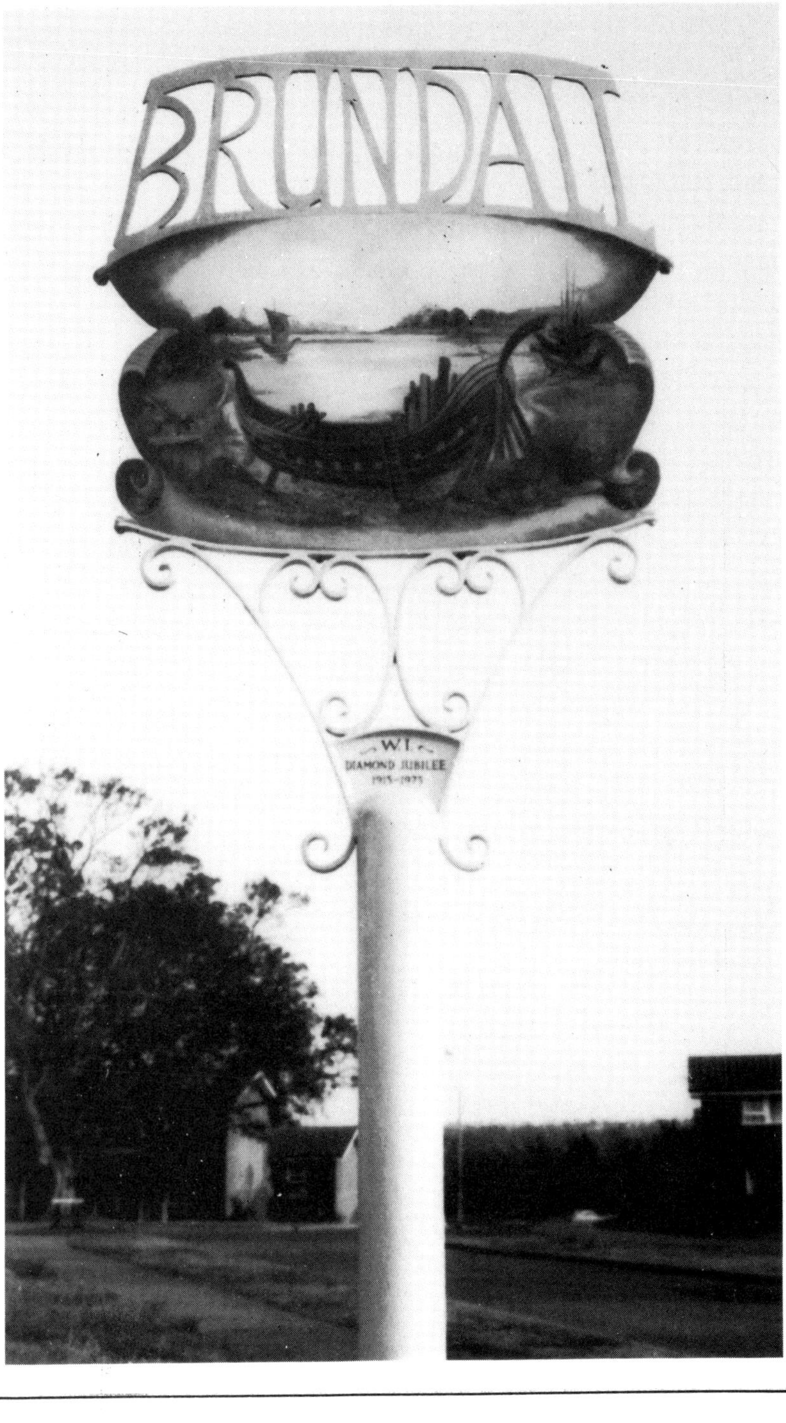
BRUNDALL
W.I.
DIAMOND JUBILEE

BURGH CASTLE

Burgh Castle was once a small village, with its nucleus around the area near the Church, but of late years it has spread considerably along the roads leading away from Breydon Water, the large estuary which was overlooked in Roman times by the great castle and the garrison it housed.

This, one of the forts of the Saxon shore, was built about 34 AD, and covered more than five acres. Its walls were fifteen feet high and some nine feet thick on three sides, the fourth side relying on the river as its western defence.

The sight of these huge flint walls and corner towers, some now leaning perilously, and silhouetted against the sky above the lonely marsh and the apparently tiny sentinel windmill far below, is something one does not easily forget.

The Village Sign, erected in the modern district, is carved in natural wood, and when we saw it was a golden chestnut in colour. Above the incised name is a representation of the mighty walls of this Roman fort, called GARIANNONUM, which can still be visted on its considerable eminence. The helmet on the ground reminds us again of the period in history so closely associated with this district.

The figure is that of St. Fursey, an early Irish Christian missionary, who came to East Anglia in the 7th century and built a monastic cell beside or within the ruins of the castle.

The Sign was designed and made by Mr. Martin Patterson of Burgh Castle and his pupils at Gorleston Grammar School. In fact part of the sign was a lid of an old school desk.

The unveiling took place in October 1976.

NEAR BURGH CASTLE

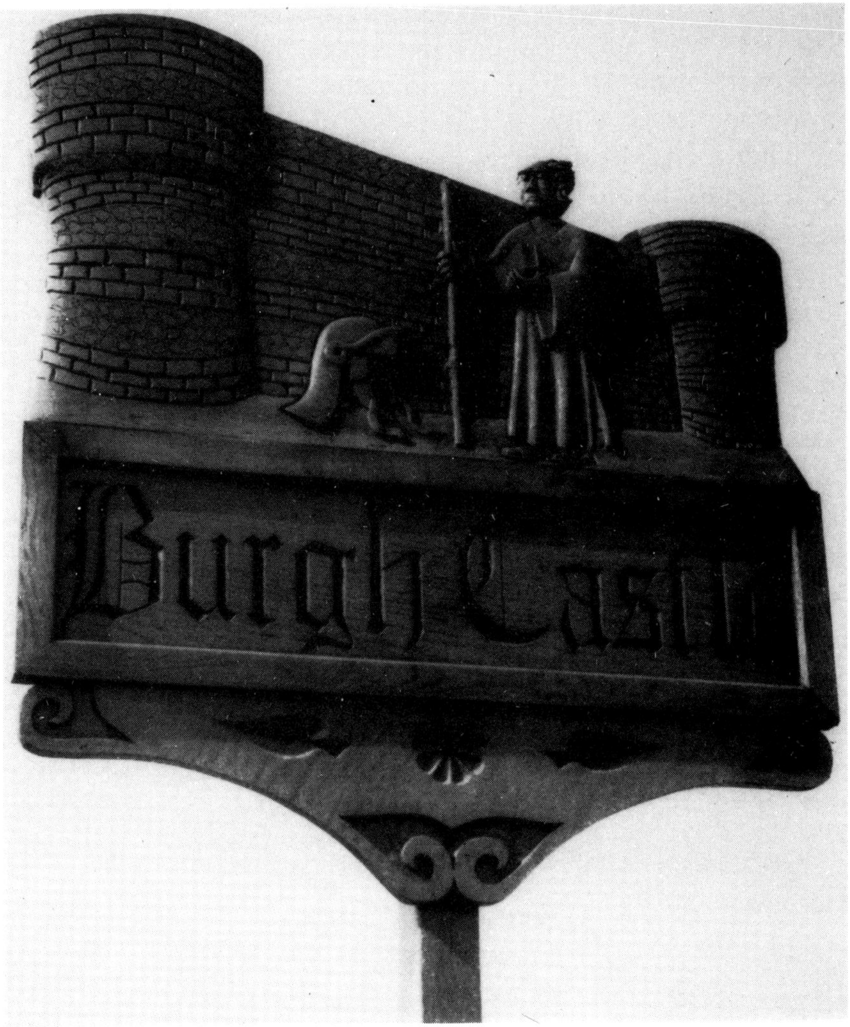
Burgh Castle

BURNHAM THORPE

There were originally seven Burnhams, not much above a mile from each other, and within easy reach of the North Norfolk coast.

Burnham Thorpe has attained distinction because it was the birthplace, in 1758, of Britain's most famous sailor, Admiral Lord Nelson. His father, Edmund Nelson, was rector here for thirty-six years, and Horatio was born in the old Rectory, which no longer exists — there is just a plaque on a wall to record the site. Many times young Horatio must have played by the little river Burn, which flows through the village and where you can see the Sign not far from a bridge.

This Sign is unique on two counts, for it was presented to the village by the Royal Navy, and it is carried out as a framed picture. The idea was suggested by the Parish Council and Lord Zuckerman, formerly the Government's chief scientific adviser, who lives here. It was made in the workshops of H.M.S. Sultan at Gosport, the Royal Navy's engineering school.

The pictured details were taken from originals presented, with other Nelsonian treasures, by an American, Mrs. L. M. McCarthy, shewing the rectory where Nelson was born and the names of famous and victorious ships and battles which contributed so much to the fame of Burnham's greatest son.

The Sign was unveiled in June 1975, and the same picture is on both sides.

BURNHAM THORPE

BURNHAM THORPE
BIRTHPLACE OF
HORATIO NELSON
29TH SEPTEMBER, 1758.

NILE
COPENHAGEN
TRAFALGAR

VANGUARD
ELEPHANT
VICTORY

BUXTON

Buxton is quite a large village with a very attractive row of cottages on the road from Norwich to Aylsham. Then an abrupt turn to the east leads one past some modern homes, the inn and the shops and to the church at the centre, thence onward by the older village street to the watermill astride the river Bure.

The Village Sign is at the road junction by the church on a tiny triangle of green. It was erected in 1977 to commemorate the Silver Jubilee of Queen Elizabeth and also the Golden Jubilee of the Women's Institute. It was presented to the village council by the Women's Institute who raised the necessary funds.

The millstone on its very solid flint base is quite unique as signs go, and is a weighty reminder of the fine large watermill at the end of the road, which was so important in the heydey of its milling life, when vast quantities of flour and animal feedstuffs were produced, largely from local grain. Since the early 70's the mill has successfully taken on a new role as a cultural art and craft centre, as well as providing a welcome restaurant.

Mr. William C. Duffield, of Buxton Mill, and the large milling concern now concentrated at Saxlingham, which bears his name, unveiled the Sign and provided the millstone, which is a French Buhr — a hard quartzite suitable for milling wheat. The grooves on the grinding surface can be seen on the east side, while the normally plain reverse side has been given a shingle coat, providing an interesting texture to offset the wrought iron letters of the name, which project an inch or so from it.

BUXTON

The large base was made by Mr. Clarke, whose family has for three generations used its building skills in the village. The Parish Council has undertaken the landscaping of the surround.

CANTLEY

Cantley has an excellent village sign. It stands at the cross roads at The Oaks Corner, just north of the village. It is erected on a bank, of about 4-5 ft. in height, so it is seen to advantage. It is well designed, every feature being well drawn and well placed.

The three churches of the parishes which combined together to erect the sign are shown in the background — Limpenhoe, Southwood, and Cantley. In Norfolk there is a great sugarbeet growing area, and the large factory at Cantley processes the huge crops produced. The factory itself can be seen for miles, but it is not unsightly. The crops are represented on the sign by the orderly rows of ploughed ground in front of the churches. (Heavily loaded lorries can be seen for months on end conveying beet to the factory to be processed into sugar as fast as it can be dealth with.) The wherry shown tells of the waterborne trading which was customary on the nearby river Yare, bound for Norwich from Yarmouth in the days before steam and petrol came into daily use and made slower means of transport obsolete, and when the very adequate wherries were abandoned in the interests of speed! There were over 200 of them in use at one time, and they must have presented a memorable sight with their great black sails moving so gracefully along our lovely inland waterways. In the right foreground of the sign are depicted some fine specimens of sugarbeet, whilst on the left are two reminders of the prolific wildlife in Norfolk, namely a shy little grebe sitting on her watery nest, and a hansome cock-pheasant disporting himself in full plumage.

There is further reason for congratulation in that the sign is entirely the work of local people. Carved in seasoned Norfolk oak, it was designed by Mr. Malcolm Wallace from the basic concept of Mr. Peter Crook, and carved by Mr. Pat Brister. This is his first village sign, and it will surely not be his last. The cost of the sign was borne by the East Anglian Real Property Company; and was erected to commemorate the Silver Jubilee of Queen Elizabeth II.

CANTLEY

LIMPENHOE　　SOUTHWOOD
CANTLEY

CARBROOKE

Carbrooke (Magna) is a small village north of the Hingham — Watton road. Opposite its church is another of Mr. Harry Carter's carvings, the Village Sign which tells of the days when the Knights Templars, and later the Knights Hospitallers, lived nearby.

A small religious house was founded in 1173 by Roger de Clare for the Templars, a military order whose members were strong and powerful and sought to assist in providing a safe passage for pilgrims visiting the Holy Land.

Later on Maud, the widow of Roger de Clare added to the endowment and gave the house to the Knights Hospitallers of St. John of Jerusalem, a religious order which cared for the travellers and the sick. The house was sometimes called the Priory or more usually the Commandery of Kerbrook — the only institution of its kind in Norfolk. The Templars had had for their badge a red cross on white, and the Hospitallers the white cross on black (N.B. our Red Cross Society and the St. John's Ambulance Service still use these).

All persons who enjoyed the privileges of this Order were allowed to fix a cross upon their houses and be exempt from tithes and other dues. This privilege, in time, was greatly abused and during the reign of Edward I had to be checked.

The sixteen stalls in the church suggest that there had been provision for a prior and fifteen knights.

At the dissolution of the monasteries in 1530 the Priory revenues were valued at £65.2.9., the house and its ancient church were granted to two knights, Sir Richard Gresham and Sir Richard Southwell. Nothing exists now above the foundations which were just south of the church.

CARBROOKE

Money for the Village Sign and its upkeep was raised by the Women's Institute.

For a short time there was a sister Commandery for nuns at Little Carbrooke but later it was abandoned and the nuns transferred to Buckland.

CORPUSTY AND SAXTHORPE

Corpusty and Saxthorpe are adjoining villages, one on each side of the River Bure, and which are linked by the bridge beside the very attractive water-mill, which, alas, is no longer working.

The two villages combined to produce their unusual Village Sign which reflects an ancient village trade. It consists of a genuine beam-type plough, made in the Saxthorpe Foundry over 100 years ago, which has been placed on a magnificent base made from red Norfolk bricks and flint cobbles. Entombed in this base (in plastic containers) are various essays and objects of the 1970s produced by the children of Corpusty Primary School. At one end of the large base is inscribed a very apt verse as follows:

The Ploughman's Prayer
The King he governs all
The Parson pray for all
The Lawyer plead for all
The Ploughman pay for all
and Feed all.

The Sign stands in a prominent position on the Corpusty side of the Village Green, between the two parishes, and was unveiled by two members of the Cornish family whose grandfather owned the above foundry.

The Sign was given by members of the Women's Institute and others who had raised the necessary £250 during the past five years. As building costs were rising faster than money was coming in, an especially great effort was made to bring the project to completion in the summer of 1974.

(CORPUSTY &) SAXTHORPE

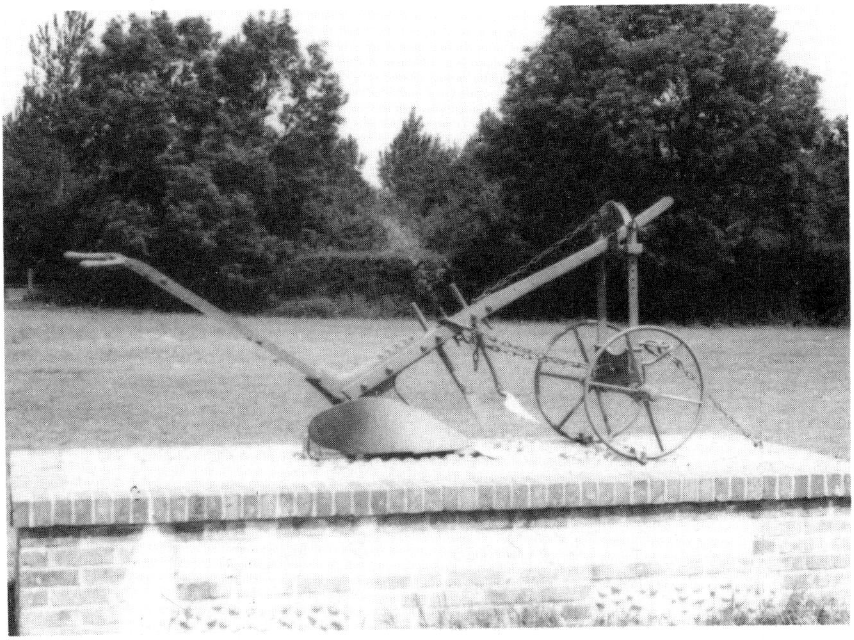

CRIMPLESHAM

About two and a half miles east from Downham Market, at the road junction which branches south towards Thetford, is the small village of Crimplesham. In May 1976 a Village Sign was put up in this village, which had previously won the "Best Kept Village" awards two years running, and the Lane family, who constructed the base, ingeniously incorporated those signs in it.

Crimplesham's Village Sign was made by Mr. Harry Carter and unveiled by the oldest parishioner, ninety-five-year-old Mr. Arthur Oakley.

A country landscape is shown with oxen pulling a plough and a flock of sheep in the foreground. Nearer still is a little river. According to the Oxford Dictionary of English Place Names, "crimple" means a crooked stream, and it is suggested that the village derived its name from that.

The whole scene is flanked by two figures, one representing Rainald, a Norman who became a tyrannical landowner in the district, and the other Ailed, who was a freewoman of the manor in medieval times.

£95, the cost of the Sign, was raised by public subscription.

CRIMPLESHAM

CRIMPLESHAM

GREAT DUNHAM

A village in which a Roman altar was unearthed in a garden needs no further evidence of its great antiquity; and since the actual site was in the rectory garden, it points to the fact that religious significance has always been associated with this particular area.

The name Dunham is derived from the Old English and means the "hamlet on the hill", or slight rise — the latter being the more applicable in this case. Great Dunham is a quiet, secluded village about two and a half miles from Litcham; and has on its green a dignified and well-designed sign, made in black ironwork. Within its attractive scroll work it bears the name Great Dunham, whilst above it, in a semicircle, it shows a very simple replica of the church. There is nothing else to give you any further information. However the most obvious thing to do is to take a look at the church itself which is only a few hundred yards along the road. In the churchyard are many magnificent elm trees, and the beautiful church is very old. Here is where we shall discover something about its village and its past, for it is these very stones which hold the key to what we want to know. Within its structure are some ancient bricks which some Anglo Saxons took from a derelict Roman building found in the vicinity, and incorporated them into the flint walls; and there is long and short work in the corners of the tower which is built between the nave and the chancel, whilst at the west end of the nave one can find a triangular Saxon doorway, which has long since been blocked in. There is further evidence of Saxon work, and of course, work of later centuries. Only a few villages can trace their origins back to such early times, and let us hope that this fine old church will have a future no less long and as secure as its past.

GREAT DUNHAM

The subject matter for the sign was suggested by a member of the local council, and Mr. Norman Pearce made a scale drawing of it. The sign was made at the Walsingham foundry. Funds came from council rates and various fund raising efforts. The stonework base was made by Mr. Reginald Thompson, a parishioner, and it was, like so many others, raised to celebrate the Queen's Silver Jubilee.

EDINGTHORPE

Here — on the way to Bacton from North Walsham — we see a very fine and striking sign standing on a small triangle of grass. It is quite clear, even from a most cursory glance that such a small community has spared no expense to show their great pride in this village of ancient origin. Its name, according to that extremely interesting mine of information "The Oxford Dictionary of English Place Names", means Eadhelm's thorpe; Eadhelm is a Saxon female name, and thorpe, or throp, comes from the Danish meaning "an out-lying dairy farm."

On the top of the sign one sees a plough; and to this day agriculture is the main industry in these parts — as it is in so much of Norfolk. In each of the small spandrels is a sheaf of corn, and the large panel is filled with a ploughing scene, with the church in the background. No more is indicated, but if you visit the church you will be well rewarded for your effort; but no incentive will be needed, for seeing the church surrounded with trees, one cannot resist going there. It must be a lovely sight, in full summer, to see the field golden with ripening corn rippling in the breeze. But in the spring it would gladden your heart to see the churchyard alive with Lent Lilies, which is the apt East Anglian name for wild daffodils. The old flint church is thatched, and is full of interest for those who will find time to visit it. Its well kept appearance, and the fact that so many things have been added to it by past generations point to the fact that Edingthorpe has always had a community of caring people.

The sign was made by Mr. Harry Carter, as a Silver Jubilee thanksgiving. Many local people contributed to the cost, as well as the Bacton and Edingthorpe Parish Council. The hearts of the Edingthorpe people must glow with pride when they look at their new sign, which is one of the most delightful signs they could wish for.

EDINGTHORPE

EDINGTHORPE

FELTHORPE

Felthorpe is a small village lying between two delightful wooded areas, favourite spots for motorists and others at nutting time, for there are many sweet chestnuts there, and incidentally two or three fine Canadian redwoods which can be seen not far away, a rare sight in Norfolk.

The Village Sign here is of an unusual shape, it was given by Mrs. Watling to the village in 1977. It is a circular drum, surmounted by a bold representation of a Royal Crown and set upon a fluted iron post. Around the drum is painted a true and attractive view of Felthorpe Hall, a white brick residence built soon after 1825. In the grounds are woods, a lake and drifts of daffodils in spring.

For nearly twenty years the Hall was the residence of Sir Basil and Lady Mayhew, including the time after Dunkirk when it became a convalescent home run by the Red Cross. Every spring vast numbers of daffodils were picked and bunched and offered for sale to raise funds for the Red Cross Society.

It seems appropriate that Felthorpe Sign is made entirely of metal, for there was a thriving business in the past concerned with the manufacture of agricultural implements. An iron founder and smith worked in the district according to Kelly's Directory of 1922.

The Sign stands near the Village Hall which was also provided by Mrs. Ruth Watling.

TO FELTHORPE WOODS

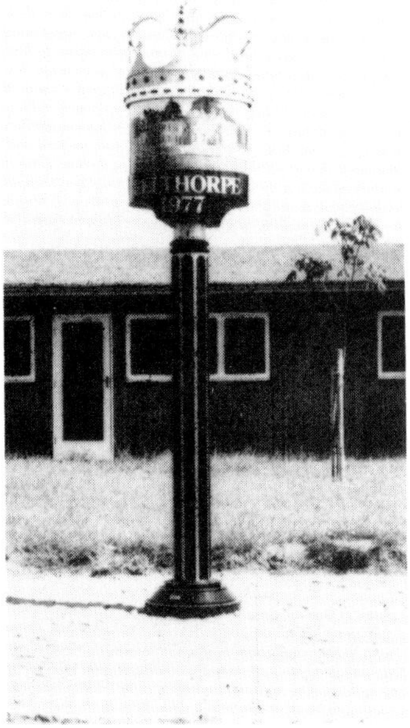
THORPE
1977

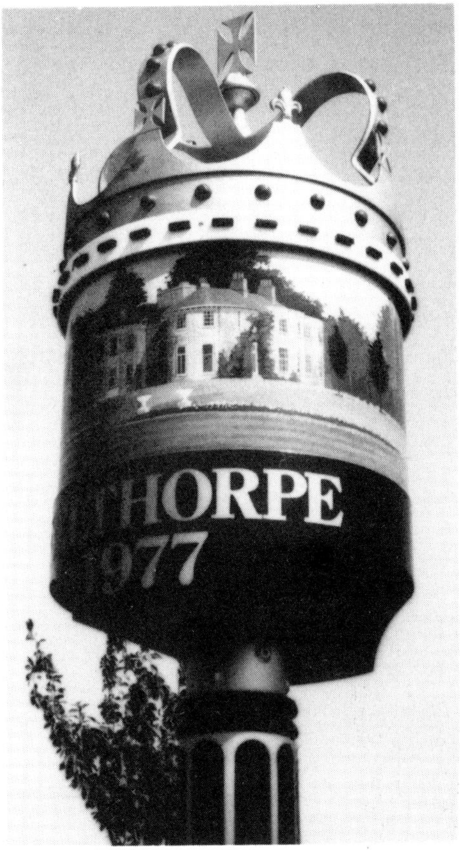
THORPE
977

FILBY

On a small green beside the main road to Yarmouth from Acle stands Filby's colourful Village Sign. The village was Danish in origin as the ending "BY", so common in this Flegg district, leads us to believe. Nearby is one of Norfolk's attractive Broads, a landlocked one and barred to motor boats.

Here it is supposed that File the Dane settled about 860 AD, and it is he depicted on the right hand side. On the left is shown Ralph de Filby, Lord of the Manor in the late 13th century, suitably clad in armour with his helm at his feet. Between them stands a stook of corn to indicate the agricultural nature of the surrounding countryside. Even the local inns are called "The Plough" and "The Jolly Farmers".

On each side of the name are two shields, those of De Warrenne and De Valence, who held lands here after the coming of William the Conqueror. On the extreme left are the arms of the notable Lucas family, one-time Lords of the Manor and whose tombs can be seen in the church, while on the right is the Cross to denote the dedication of the church to All Saints.

Below the name are two more shields, the top one being the arms of the Filbys and the lower one is the symbol given to East Anglian's martyred St. Edmund.

The sign was put up in September 1976, and it was the work of Mr. Harry Carter, and Mr. Peter Chapman who lives in the village was responsible for the design. Funds were raised by public donations. It has an attractive and sturdy brick and flint base.

It is rather intriguing to note that a society has been formed, the idea being mooted by Mr. Elsworth **Filby** from Kansas when he was on holiday in England. In June 1977 preparations were going ahead for the 4th reunion of anyone with a surname resembling Filby or Philby. Hundreds of Filbys turned up from Britain, the U.S.A. and Australia even at the first meeting in 1968, and much research has been done by the Association, locating records of over 3000 births (since 1837) registered in the name of Filby.

FILBY BROAD

1975

FILBY

FRAMINGHAM EARL

Two villages some five miles south-east of Norwich are, as it were, interlocked, Framingham Pigot thrusting into the back of Framingham Earl. In 1234 a Ralph Picot held the former, but the latter refers to the Earl of Norfolk (see the "Oxford Dictionary of English Place-Names").

Framingham Earl has its Village Sign in a commanding position on the main Norwich to Bungay road.

The village has at least two claims to fame. Firstly its wealth of fine forest trees was planted by an eminent surgeon named Edward Rigby, who practised in Norwich for fifty-three years. He was also Mayor of that city in 1805, and worked hard to introduce vaccination, as well as being interested in improvements in agriculture.

There is a tombstone in the churchyard to Dr. Edward Rigby, and on it is written

"A monument to Rigby do you seek,
On everyside the whisp'ring woodlands speak."

Secondly, the Saxon-Norman Church of St. Andrew has rich and ornately carved arches and doorways, and is renowned for the enormous flints used as cornerstones in the nave.

Both these facts are recorded in the very attractive Sign which was designed and painted by Mrs. Sheila Michalski. It is carried out in pierced and wrought metal, and was unveiled by the Bishop of Thetford, a former parishioner of Framingham Earl, in March 1976.

FRAMINGHAM EARL

FRAMINGHAM EARL

HAPPISBURGH

Happisburgh is a long village extending from the church in the north to the equally familiar landmark — the banded lighthouse in the south. It nestles below a ridge, culminating in high cliffs, parallel to the windswept coast of north-east Norfolk. As you approach from Bacton and turn abruptly south below Happisburgh church on its hill, you see immediately, in a little bay set into a sunwarmed wall, the Village Sign which was erected in the autumn of 1976.

It stands on a platform facing the road and screened from bitter easterly gales by a bank of trees. The arch shape suggests the interior of the church and in the centre, behind the font, stands the parson baptising children.

It is recorded that in 1793 the Reverend Thomas Lloyd was concerned because so few of his poorer parishioners came forward to have their children baptised, partly, he felt, because they could not afford the subsequent festivites which were customary. So he offered to all who brought their children for baptism on Whitsunday, entertainment afterwards. That day 120 were baptised!

The figures on the left and right remind us of earlier events. Many of our villages date from before the Norman conquest, and Happisburgh (pronounced Haisboro') is one. On the right is Edric the Dane who was overlord here in the 11th century, and on the left is Maud, a daughter of Roger Bigod who had received the gift of this manor from the king. She married William D'Albini, one of William's knights, who founded in 1107 Wymondham Abbey. When she died she was thought to have been buried here. Four priors and a bishop attended her funeral.

Also shown on the sign is a typical early lifeboat as well as the church and lighthouse already mentioned. On the shield are ears of wheat suggesting the cornfields on the landward side of the village.

The sign was made by Mr. Harry Carter and the cost borne by the efforts of various village societies.

HAPPISBURGH

HAPPISBURGH

One would suppose that as time passed by it would be hard to find an original idea for a village sign — something that had not been thought of before. But Norfolk is rich in resources, for when Mrs. Heather Seager was researching into Hempnall's past, she made the discovery that in 1759 the famous Evangelist John Wesley came to Hempnall to preach. Now it so happens that Mrs. Seager is a descendant of Susannah Wesley — a sister of John Wesley; so in this way the main theme was decided upon.

In John Wesley's Journal he made this entry, which is recorded on the sign. "The ringleader of the mob came with his horn, as usual, before I began, but one quickly catched and threw away his horn, and in a few minutes he was deserted by all his companions who were seriously attentive to the great truth, 'By grace ye are saved through faith.' " Then the work went ahead; the task of making the sign was given to Mr. Stan Girling of Mulbarton, teacher of metal work at Long Stratton Modern Secondary School. Mr. Malcom Dye, of Hempnall Green presented an old oak post from a church on which to mount it. The coveted site on which to erect it, in the centre of the village, was occupied by a telephone box — a problem which was soon disposed of by the Parish Council, who paid to have it removed to a more suitable position. Lastly this very attractive sign, which was carried out in black and gold, and was set in a large suitable base around which a seat was constructed by Mr. Philip Becket, who made it from flint and brick from an old mill in the village.

So if you come to see this unusual sign in this delightful village, which is about ten miles south of Norwich, you will approach it through pretty, pastoral country, but it is most **unlikely** that you will go there and back on foot as John Wesley did!

HEMPNALL

The sign shows John Wesley under a large tree waiting to preach to a group of people, including the heckler, with his horn, ready to create a disturbance.

The sign was a gift from the Hempnall Women's Institute, to commemorate the Queen's Silver Jubilee.

HEMPTON GREEN

Hempton Green, a parish on the outskirts of Fakenham, once had a Priory (at Abbey Farm) which had been founded by Roger de St. Martin in the reign of Henry I, for Augustinian canons, as a hospital.

At the time of the Dissolution there were only four canons and the revenues were £39.0.9.

Hempton, however, was more famous for its common which provided a large pasturage, as much as sixty-eight acres! Cattle fairs were held there two or three times a year and in the 18th century cattle were brought from as far away as Scotland, walking the whole distance of course. The Sheep Fair on the first Wednesday in September was held for the last time in 1969 — a large gathering on a lovely day.

On the Village Sign, made by Mr. Harry Carter, and unveiled by Marquess Townshend (Lord of the Manor) and which was given by the Women's Institute, we see depicted part of the old Priory ruins, a monk, and cattle and sheep with their drovers in the foreground.

On the reverse side, the little train recalls the old days when the Eastern and Midland Railway linked King's Lynn and Fakenham. Only a short length of old platform is still visible from the road into Fakenham.

The base of the Sign, built by Mr. Gant, includes flints gathered from the old Priory site by members of the Women's Institute.

Hamatuna was the name recorded in the Domesday Book of the 11th century for this Parish.

HEMPTON GREEN

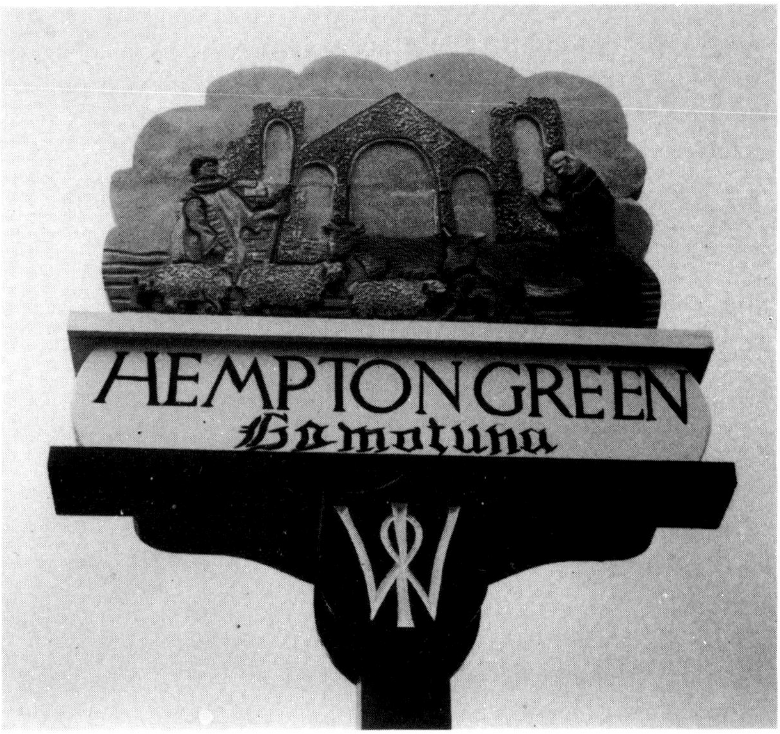
HEMPTON GREEN

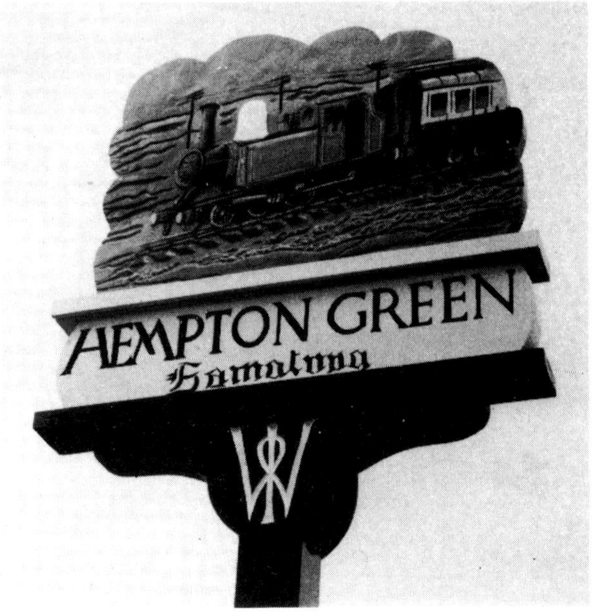
HEMPTON GREEN

HETHERSETT

Hethersett, once typical of a fairly large village with its main street between the Queen's Head and the King's Head, (the latter still a very attractive inn) and with other houses along the minor roads leading westward, has recently expanded enormously with several acres of modern development.

The new by-pass, the A11, skirts it all, except for the church, Hall and a nearby farm, which are severed from the rest by a constant stream of speeding traffic.

The Village Sign was carved in natural oak and treated with oil. It looked very splendid when it was unveiled in 1974.

A competition had been set to design the Sign, suggested by the local Women's Institute in collaboration with the Village Council, and Mr. Mapes produced the winning entry, in which he had been helped by Mr. Nairn's research. Mr. Mapes then offered to carve the sign itself, a very welcome voluntary effort in which he was supported by Mr. Burrell who provided a base of two tiers of brick and stone slabs.

On the Sign are three things, a replica of the 14th century Church of St. Remigius, a deer to denote the original name "Hederseta", meaning an enclosure for deer, and a stylised carving of a tree, with oak leaf and acorn thereon to record the continued existence of the famous old oak on the border of the parish, which, it is said, was the meeting place of Robert Kett and his adherents in 1549. This Wymondham tanner and his followers rebelled against the enclosure of common lands and marched on Norwich. After initial success the rebellion was crushed and the leaders hanged.

HETHERSETT

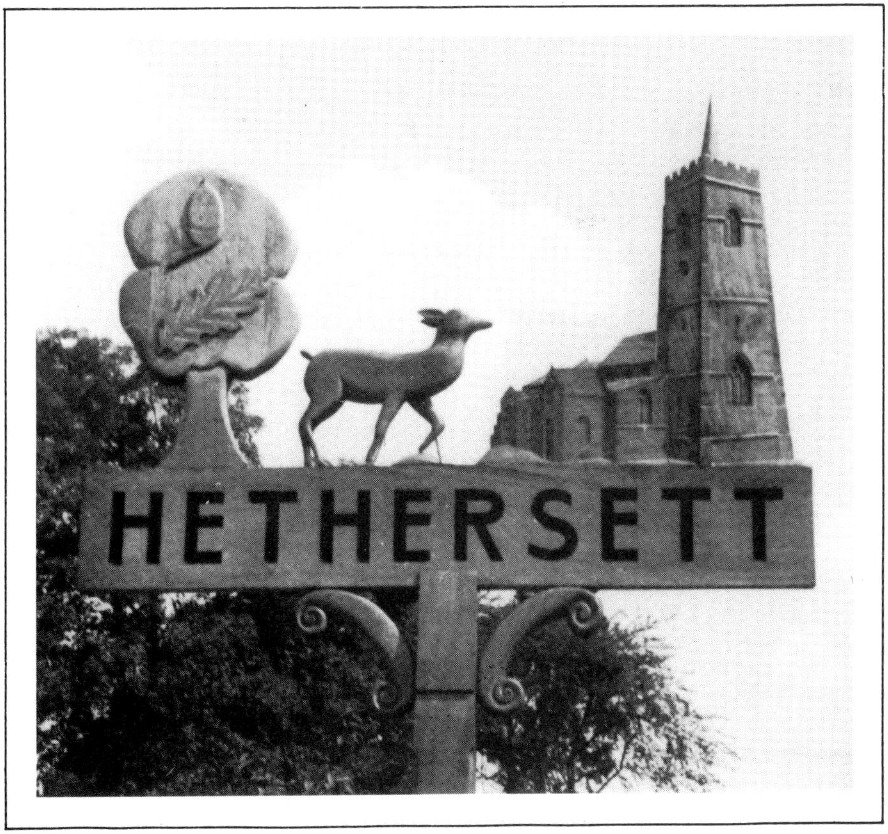
HETHERSETT

HEVINGHAM

At Hevingham there is a Sign of two crossed birch brooms which recalls a staple industry of the village in the past.

Today many great tree-trunks lie in the local woodyards, indicating the proximity of park and plantations, which can be seen especially in the south of the parish. At least two of the yards supply the mining industry with pit-props. Why, we wonder, does part of this parish possess the delightful name of Cats-cum-Cricketots?

The background of the Sign fits with the description given by the Reverend Francis Blomfield when he wrote about the village in 1750, mentioning that it lay at the confluence of several tiny streams. In the distance beyond a stream is shown the church which actually is a mile or so away on the main road between Norwich and Aylsham.

The idea of the Sign was conceived by Mr. Wymer, one of the last of the brushmakers, and given by the Women's Institute. It was made by Mr. Harry Carter and handed over to Mr. Walter Medler, Chairman of the Parish Council. It is interesting to note that in Kelly's Directory of 1888 a Samuel Medler was mentioned as a broom-maker.

The Sign has been placed at the corner of an attractive green at Westgate, the north west corner of the village.

HEVINGHAM

HEVINGHAM

HICKLING

Hickling Broad is a well known boating centre and a nature reserve. It can be approached by road only in the vicinity of the popular Pleasure Boat Inn, at which so many cruisers call when their occupants are enjoying holidays on the Norfolk Broads. The vast expanse of open water provides superb opportunities for sailing, while the lonely creeks and organised hides are havens for bird watchers.

The village straggles somewhat, from the church in the north, as the road wanders in a southerly direction through Hickling Green and diverges towards the Broad.

The Village Sign, which stands in a good central position, was presented by the parishioners in 1974. On it is carved a representation of the ancient Priory, for which Hickling was renowned in the past, while on the roundels below the name are depicted the Swallowtail butterfly, which breeds only in Norfolk, and that rare bird, the Bittern, which nests in the reed beds of the district — the result of careful nature conservation of recent years. Also shown on the other side are reed cutting for thatching, and peat digging as in the past.

Below the name, on an oak post, is a replica of a thirteen century seal from the Priory which says, "Behold the Seal of St. Mary of Hickling".

Theobald de Valoins founded the Priory in 1185, and four canons from the Augustinian Priory at St. Osyth came to instruct the Hickling canons in the rule of their Order.

HICKLING BROAD

By 1291 Hickling Priory had been granted possessions in no fewer than 32 parishes. The canons who were ordained priests lived a common life and owned no property. Markets were held there and the Priory existed for 351 years, surviving a great flood and the Black Death. Some ruined portions of the Priory can be seen today well north of the church.

The Sign was designed and made by Mr. Harry Carter, and the base by Mr. W. Lambert of Hickling, in which he used flints from a churchyard wall. It was unveiled by Mr. J. C. Cadbury who was instrumental in acquiring Whiteslea Reserve for the Norfolk Naturalists' Trust.

HOCKWOLD cum WILTON

The villages of Hockwold and Wilton lie a few miles north of Brandon, in the south west of our county and have become literally one settlement.

The Sign was erected as a gift to the parishioners through public subscription in 1973-4. Mr. Harry Carter made it, and the plinth is built of local flints in which an original WILTON brick was embedded. The site was leased at the nominal rent of 5p a year by the Hockwold Village Working Men's Club and Institute.

There are many interesting aspects of the past incorporated in this sign (which is difficult to photograph as it faces due north). A sunny landscape with the Church of St. James and its rare 14th century spire belongs to Wilton, and the interior of the church is rich in carved woodwork. On the right is the now redundant Church of St. Peter, Hockwold. The stream depicts the Little Ouse, which was the southern boundary of the parishes and the county. In the foreground are carvings of a hare, greyhounds and their handler, to recall the activities of the widely known Hockwold Coursing Club (1920–1939).

Below the name plate are three devices. Loaves of bread denote an early Charity when six loaves were provided weekly for six poor Protestants. Three beehives recall the 17 mentioned in the Domesday Book, and the acorns represent the "Pannage for 200 hogs and 30 goats". Finally the chequerboard pattern symbolises the arms of the Earl de Warrenne (1086) who held much land in this area.

Only a few weeks after the unveiling of this sign it disappeared! The villagers were rightly angry, but eventually the culprit was discovered to be an American airman, whose joke went awry, and who was heavily fined. The sign was returned and repaired, and valued at the time at about £200.

HOCKWOLD

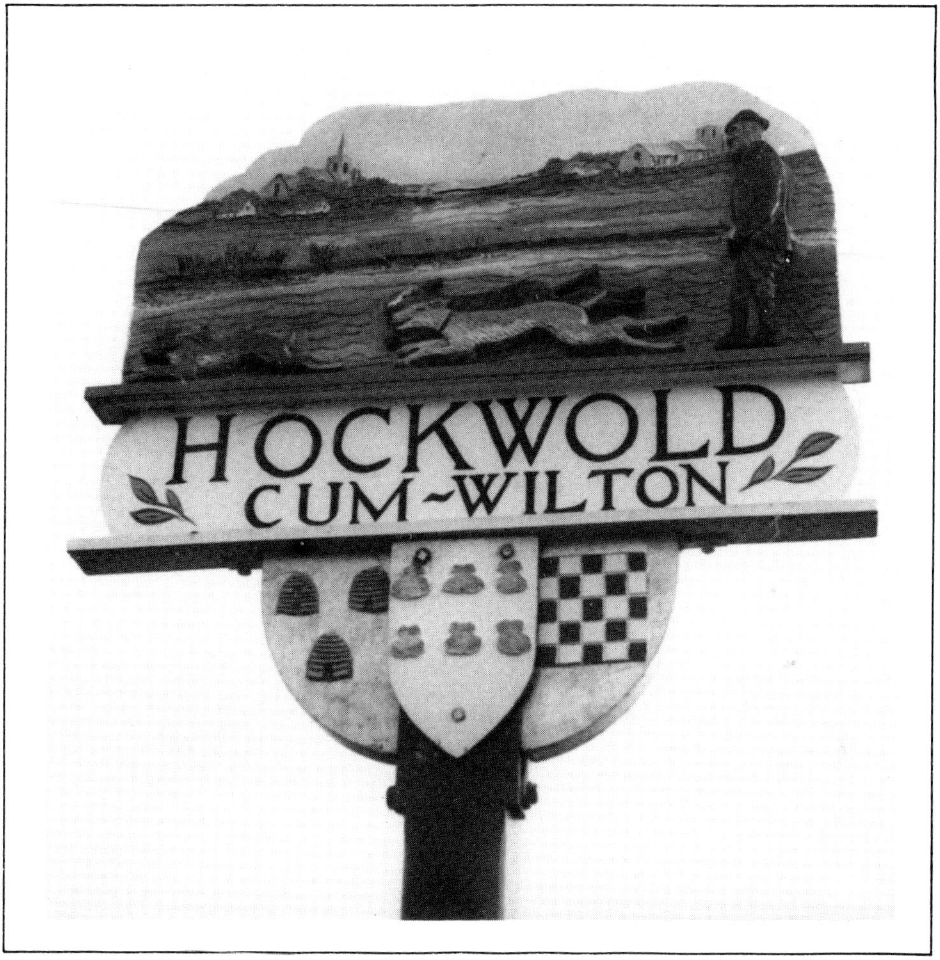
HOCKWOLD
CUM-WILTON

HOLT

Holt is an attractive and compact little market town within easy reach of such well-known seaside resorts as Sheringham, Blakeney and Wells. Much of its charm is due to its 18th century character, for most of the town was rebuilt after a disastrous and all-consuming fire in 1708.

Holt's Town Sign, erected in 1976 in front of Barclay's Bank, records two outstanding characters closely connected with the town, one very famous and the other? — well, infamous is the better word. Another and amusing reminder of Holt's past is also recorded here. An owl was once captured and put for safety into the market "pound"! — which is possibly why the people of the town, and a football club too, are known as Holt Owls (or know-alls) today.

But to return to the famous man, gay in his Tudor costume, depicted on the side which faces the street. He was one of the four sons of James Gresham, who all went to London and were in business there.

John became financial agent to Wolsey, and later was made Lord Mayor of London and knighted. It was this Sir John Gresham who founded the free grammar school in Holt in 1554, and six years later it was opened under the trusteeship of the Worshipful Company of Fishmongers, for Sir John had died of the plague just before. "Gresham's" is still, of course, a school of considerable repute.

On the inner side of Holt Sign is shown Alice Perers who entered the service of Queen Philippa in the 14th century, and although she later married Sir Thomas Nerford she became the mistress of King Edward III.

After the death of Sir Thomas Nerford and of the Queen, Edward presented his mistress with his wife's jewels and other property! But Alice was considered a

HOLT

corrupt influence at court and was banished eventually by the Black Prince, and her property was confiscated. However, later she regained Royal favour, and in time, three more husbands! Her great attraction seemed not in her personal charms, but in her ability to excel in the art of flattery.

Was it coincidence that the Manor House of Holt-Perers was the original home of Gresham's School? Actually Sir John had bought it from his brother who had become the owner, for the purpose of making it a school.

The money for the Sign, which was made by Mr. Harry Carter, was raised by the efforts of the town's two Women's Institutes, the Holt Afternoon W.I. and the Holt Owls W.I., in June 1976. It stands on a very impressive stepped base.

HORSFORD

Horsford lies about five miles north of Norwich. It is a very long village, stretching about a mile or even further. It has grown much during recent years, and looks thriving and progressive with its modern houses and bungalows happily placed amongst older buildings. Horsford is also an old village, and is mentioned in Domesday Book; it includes a manor house, an old church, a windmill of later date, and a dignified Georgian hall — or house.

Its delightful and impressive sign stands on what is known as Crown Hill, and is to be seen as one enters the village approaching it from Norwich. The name Horsford lends itself to a rebus, so it requires no explanation when one sees a picture of a manor house in the background, whilst in front of it there is a horse drinking at a ford, which strikes the eye very pleasantly. On the reverse side is shown a representation of a beautiful window in the church which was placed there as a memorial to three sisters, all of whom died tragically of consumption within eighteen months of each other whilst barely out of their "teens". One really should make a visit to the church to see the original stained glass window, which was painted by a very gifted artist, named Zetler, of Munich. Facing south, a warm light shines through it, showing in a scene of mingled Egyptian and Swiss scenery, three angelic figures. The scenery is to record their journeys to more genial climates, in their search for a cure from this dreadful disease (from which they eventually, and so pathetically died). The exquisite rendering of the Swiss flowers cannot fail to delight all wild flower lovers. The family once lived in the Hall opposite the church. The rest of the sign depicts in the spandrels the local industries which were carried on in the past: these were weaving, milling, brickmaking, and flag-cutting — an older local name for peat-cutting. The peat was sent to London for fuel.

HORSFORD

The sign was made by Mr. Harry Carter, and was unveiled by Lady Barrett-Lennard to commemorate the Golden Jubilee of the Horsford afternoon branch of the Women's Institute. Members of the Barrett-Lennard family have been Lords of the Manor since the Norman Conquest, and only left the district a few years ago, which is surely a long tenure!

A coat of arms surmounts the sign, and several others of the Barrett-Lennard family are to be found in the church.

The base of the sign was constructed by Mr. Brian Childerhouse, who included in it flints from a local demolished wall.

There are some slight and unrecorded remains of an ancient castle in the district, worthy of research and a "dig" by some interested and enterprising archaeologists of the future.

HORSHAM and NEWTON ST. FAITH
(commonly known as Horsham St. Faith)

Many of Norfolk's village signs are given by Women's Institutes; but funds have to be raised to pay for them; and in the case of smaller groups, as this one is, it sometimes takes a considerable time to achieve. At Horsham St. Faith it took five years of sustained effort to collect enough money to pay for their sign, but it must be conceded that their labours have resulted in the production of a very handsome one which enhances still further their beautiful village. It glows with colour, and photographers will find it a good subject to record.

On the south side of the sign St. Faith is depicted with a trail of roses around her. These refer to the lovely "Garden of Remembrance" in the nearby crematorium grounds, where roses grow in profusion; and also to the acres of roses cultivated by Morse Bros. — rose growers, in a field close to the church. The small Tudor rose refers to Catherine Howard, the ill-fated young wife of King Henry VIII; who stayed at the priory when she was a ward of her uncle, the Duke of Norfolk. On the top of the sign is a replica of the priory which was founded in A.D. 1105, and dedicated by Robert Fitzwalter, Lord of the Manor, and his wife Sybil to St. Faith as a thank offering to her for her miraculous intervention enabling them to escape from brigands whilst returning from a pilgrimage to Rome. In the remains of the priory, now incorporated in a house, some fine medieval wall-paintings may be seen, which, among other things illustrate their journey. The priory was dissolved in A.D. 1536.

On the reverse side of the sign is shown a picture of a man weaving. This refers to two distinct periods when weaving was an important industry in the village. The first was in the sixteenth century when some Flemish weavers settled here, and later in the nineteenth and early twentieth century when the weaving of horsehair cloth was a thriving trade.

HORSHAM ST FAITHS

The work of making and carving it was entrusted to Mr. Harry Carter; and the imposing base of bricks and flint was constructed by Mr. Michael Green. Mr. John Woods gave the Westmorland Slate slab on which Mr. Charlie Taylor did the lettering. Mr. Newall donated a priory stone, and Dr. Eve and Mr. Mapsted gave the flints.

OLD HUNSTANTON

Old Hunstanton is one of the most attractive seaside places in East Anglia. It retains much of its old character, and in addition it has invigorating air, a sandy curving beach, and most dramatic looking red and white chalk cliffs, standing on a base of brown and yellow carstone.

The village sign is very original in subject matter and delightful in appearance. It tells the story of an old tradition in the L'Estrange (also spelled "le Strange") family who owned and occupied Hunstanton Hall for more than 400 years, but who were unfortunately obliged to relinquish it in 1948 when heavy taxation made it impossible to maintain it any longer. It has a fine entrance gateway made by Inigo Jones. Sad to relate, owing to a disastrous fire, the right hand side of the hall is now only a hollow shell. On the sign the hall forms the background for the figure of a horse-borne man who carries a javelin or spear. This was probably the Roger L'Estrange who built the hall, and of whom an exceptionally fine portrait brass is to be found in the church. The head of the L'Estrange family held the hereditary title of Lord High Admiral of the Wash. His estate extended to the foreshore and his office of Lord High Admiral gave him the right to claim possession of anything out to sea for as far as a man on a horse could throw a spear. On the sign we see him ready to establish his ownership. Also are to be seen in the spandrels, the arms of the le Strange family, and the emblem of the Women's Institute.

This pleasing sign is mounted on a fine plinth of brick and flint; and it stands on the main coast road at the junction of Sea Lane.

It was presented by the Old Hunstanton Women's Institute who erected it to commemorate the occasion of the Queen's Silver Jubilee. It was made by Mr. Harry Carter, and the plinth was constructed by Mr. Tony Richardson — a local builder.

HUNSTANTON

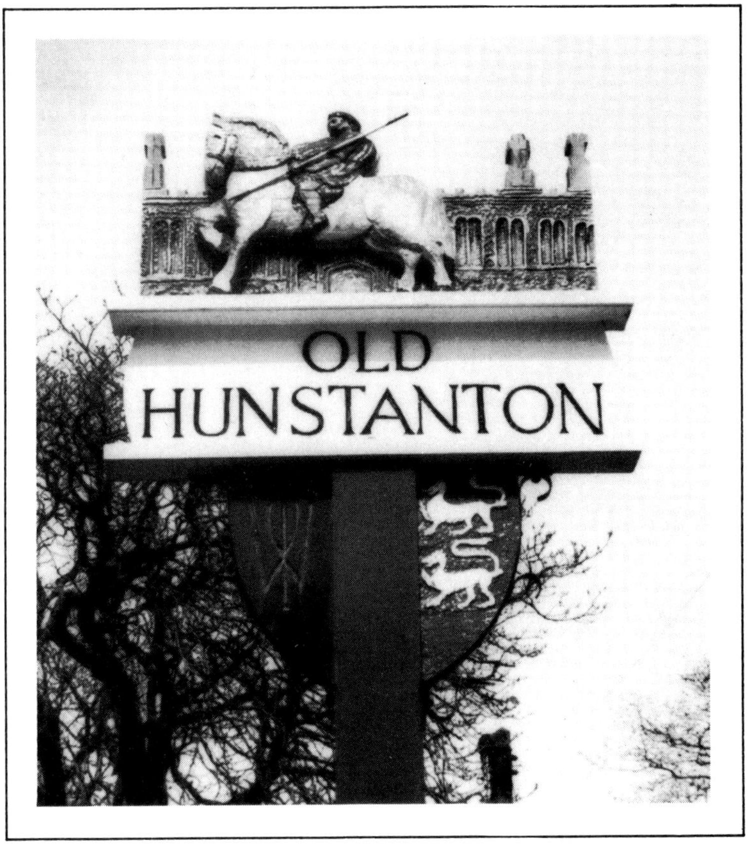
OLD
HUNSTANTON

THE LEXHAMS

Within a few miles east of Castle Acre, are to be found the two villages of West and East Lexham, which lie about two miles apart; and each of them has a village sign, which is delightful to look at, and was made by Mr. Harry Carter.

38 EAST LEXHAM

On entering East Lexham one is surprised to see on the small green made by the junction of three roads, a small structure which looks like a butter-cross such as is seen in Wymondham and Aylsham, and as far away as Dunster in Somerset, and Abbots Bromley, in Staffordshire.

These were built many years ago, under them was sold farm and dairy produce; but this one, at East Lexham is probably less than 100 years old; so its purpose is somewhat problematical, nevertheless its appearance is most attractive, and is also enhanced by a very intriguing weather vane, which is sure to command admiration. Some of the few houses are old, and the total effect is delightful.

It is under the cover of this butter-cross that the attractive sign is erected, and although this protective covering may greatly prolong the lifespan of the sign, it does, unfortunately, obscure it somewhat, and makes photography very difficult without flash.

The sign is two-sided, and illustrates farming as it was many centuries ago, and now is, owing to the great advance in modern mechanical methods, using machinery. So on one side there is a picture of a simple plough being driven as in Saxon times; whilst on the other a modern version is juggernauting on its way, regardless of terrain, but ruthlessly efficient! And this comparison is appropriately stressed by a visit to the parish church which has so many Saxon features in it,

EAST LEXHAM

as to make the slight journey to it imperative to all who are interested in architecture; it is without a doubt worth going many miles to see it.

Lexham thus presents an impression of Norfolk in years gone by, before the necessity for adopting modern farming methods robbed us of so much that is pleasant and precious to see in our lovely county of Norfolk.

WEST LEXHAM

Actually West Lexham is little more than a hamlet, set in the heart of farming country, with an ancient church, a large and prosperous looking farm, and some pretty cottages and houses. Its peaceful appearance is most striking and satisfying to the eye. Its sign, which stands on a high bank beside the road, and backed with trees, strikes the keynote of its appeal, by showing a picture of an aspect of West Lexham itself. It is perfectly recognisable from a road above the church. It comprises a happy farming scene, whilst in front of the branches of the trees across the top are to be seen two pheasants in flight. In the two spandrels below are to be found a pigeon and an owl. The sign stands on a well constructed base of brick and flint.

In its entirety West Lexham seems like a place untouched by time, only its church bears witness to the passage of years.

The two villages are linked by a lovely road winding its way through charming, wooded pastoral country, which after turning to cross the river Nar reaches East Lexham.

WEST LEXHAM

WEST LEXHAM

WEST LYNN

West Lynn is a busy and extensive suburb of its neighbour across the water — King's Lynn, and winds its way towards the west bank of the Ouse, and to Ferry Square, which is a picturesque corner with a fine view of Lynn's waterfront.

West Lynn's Sign was presented by the Women's Institute in 1972, and the local council agreed to be responsible for its upkeep. It was placed where the road branches East, away from the busy main road from King's Lynn to the Fens and the North. It shows the Church of St. Peter, and one of the great cedar trees which had become quite famous. St. Peter himself is shewn, with his staff and his keys, walking along the edge of the quay, below which is a boat used in the past, and now, to ferry people across the river, to and from the royal town of Lynn.

The carving was done by a well-known local man, Mr. A. A. Bailey, who incidentally also carved the detailed and dignified one for King's Lynn itself, which was sited at the western end of the great iron marshland river bridge a mile or so upstream.

WEST LYNN
FERRY SQUARE

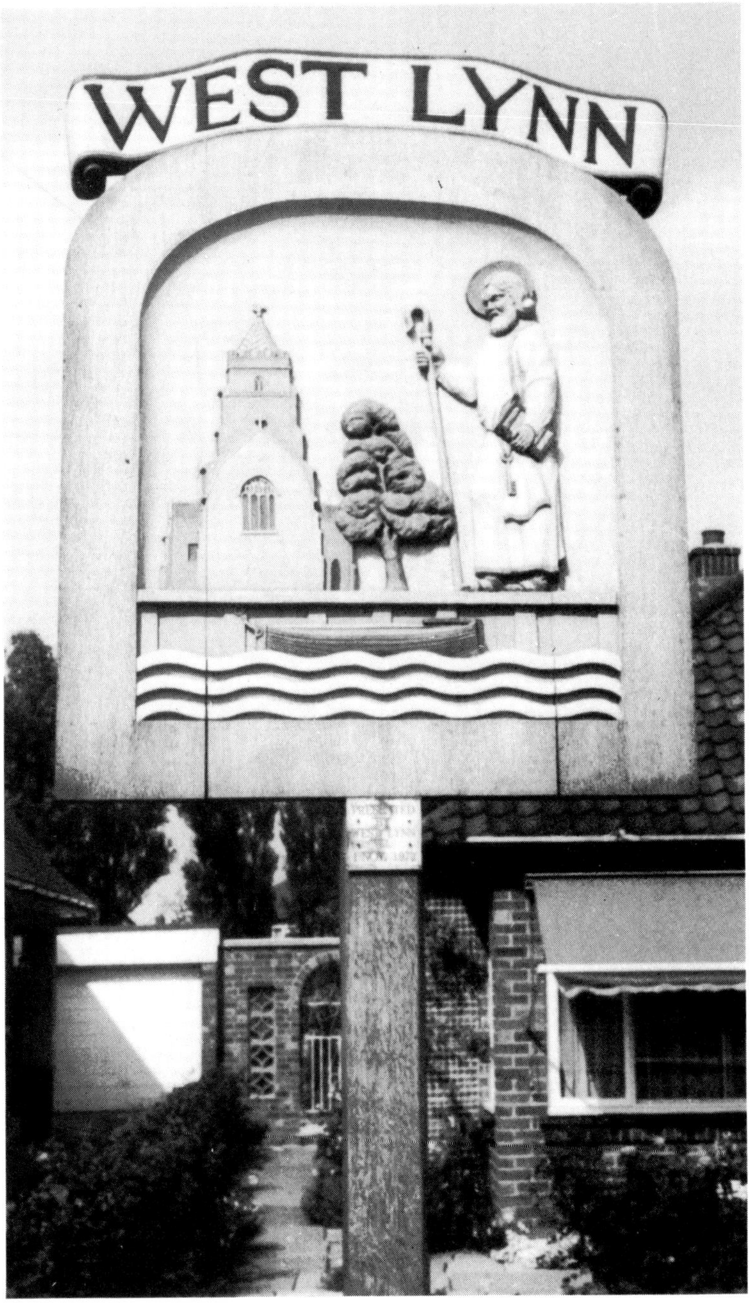
WEST LYNN

MARHAM

Marham is a village, as it were, in two sections, built mainly along a road about one and a half miles long. Many of its older buildings and walls are built entirely of the hard chalk (or clunch) from the local quarries. It even has a tomb in the church with the effigies carved in chalk.

Within its parish boundaries is an important R.A.F. station, unobtrusively set well back from the road. Marham is mentioned in Domesday Book; the name is derived from the Old English and means "the hamlet by the mere", but the mere dried up centuries ago.

In the village, close to the parish church — well worth a visit — stands the striking, and impressive village sign, which one can see even at a glance is very informative. This sign was the generous gift of the R.A.F. station to their host village, which must have felt very gratified to be the recipient of such a coveted possession; for the cost of a sign often takes years of work before a small community is able to afford one.

Opposite the church there was, a long time ago, a nunnery of the Cistercian order, of which some slight remains may be seen. It was founded in A.D. 1249 and dedicated to Saints Mary, Barbara and Edmund; it was dissolved when so many others were, in the reign of King Henry VIII.

On the sign the large panel shows a stylised picture of a nun named after St. Barbara, who is said to have been killed at the dissolution, and whose ghost is sometimes seen in the vicinity. Also there are four panels, each bearing on other points of interest in Marham. The plough, of course, represents agriculture which is still the main industry in the district. The aeroplane is a reference to the flying activities from an older airfield here; another panel shows the buildings and chimney of a pumping station which carries the excellent drinking water found rising in this chalky district, to Wisbech, March, etc. The cherries refer to the time when Marham was known as Cherry Marham on account of the large and luscious cherries which grew here in profusion, whilst its sea of blossom in the Spring was a memorable sight.

MARHAM

The eagle at the top, we understand, is the crest of an important family and it can be seen in the church.

The sign was made by Mr. Harry Carter, who also made the beautiful emblem of the R.A.F. which stands in the precincts of their station. The plinth and post were provided by donations from the village, and the unveiling ceremony was to mark the Queen's Silver Jubilee.

MARTHAM

Martham, on the main road between Acle and Winterton, is a large and attractive village where many houses encircle an extensive green, and with a shopping centre in a second open space around the pond, where families of ducks disport themselves. The road, which passes through both, leads to the fine church and on to the coast.

Martham Sign was put up in October 1975 and is very well placed on the corner of the central green. It is double-sided and shows two colourful scenes. On the west side can be seen a representation of the fine Gothic Church of St. Mary high above the river on which is a Viking ship. In the foreground a Viking warrior advances on a British defender and his wife who is pleading for mercy. It is well known that the Danes swept across the eastern fringes of Norfolk, raiding and plundering at first, and then later settling in this district of Flegg.

On the other side there is a typical trading wherry, a familiar sight before and around the turn of the century and up to the 1914-1918 war, sailing perhaps between Norwich and Yarmouth and the more remote villages, taking grain and bringing coal or wood and other commodities to and from this "hill-top" town at the head of the river Thurne.

A wherry is a long shallow craft peculiar to the Norfolk rivers and Broads, and unique in its simple and ingenious rig, (the wherryman is beginning to lower the sail), also in its ability to sail very close to the wind, and therefore to navigate the endless changes of direction in the winding reaches of the rivers. Behind the wherry is a tower windmill used to pump water from the marshes and make it possible to use them for cattle-grazing. It stands on the embankment behind the typical line of reeds.

MARTHAM

The Sign, once more the work of Mr. Harry Carter, was given to the village by the Parish Council, and a local builder Mr. Harris generously provided the base and surround.

MELTON CONSTABLE

At each end of Melton Constable can be found a framed print of an engine of the Midland and Great Northern Joint Railway, most apt and suitable to be the Sign of this one-time railway boom town.

In the middle of the 19th century Melton Constable was a small village, in fact after several people had emigrated there were, in 1841, only seventy-five inhabitants!

However when the railroads were beginning to penetrate the county, the great landowners, seeing the advantages such transport would bring to the region, invested their money and business acumen in the development of the railway network. Such men as L'Estrange of Hunstanton and Upcher of Sheringham were instrumental in creating seaside resorts from what were once small fishing communities.

The Lord of the Manor, Lord Hastings of Melton Hall provided construction and repair sheds, and gave up part of his land for the line to pass through. He built rows of terraced houses for the workers to live in and Melton Constable soon grew into a town once called the "Crewe of Norfolk".

Below the painting of the engine — golden in colour — to suggest the acres of gorse by the East Coast towns it linked, is the name and a coat of arms, quartered to show the major centres Peterborough, Norwich' Lynn and Yarmouth. On the surrounding garter is the inscription "The Midland and Great Northern Joint Railway". The obvious growth and prosperity of Melton in the railway's heyday was eventually checked, presumably by Dr. Beeching's axe. Then perhaps the railway really deserved the unkind translation of M & G N as the "Muddle and Get Nowhere" line.

MELTON CONSTABLE

These Signs were put up in 1975, the Diamond Jubilee year of the local Women's Institute.

It is interesting to note that some of the early Lords of the Manor of Melton held the office of Constable in the service of the Bishop of Thetford, the original owner after the Conquest, and sometimes styled themselves Melton de Constable, hence the name we know today.

MILEHAM

Mileham is a village scattered along a main road from North Elmham to Litcham and King's Lynn.

Some slight remains of a motte and bailey castle can still be seen in a field behind the sign. The castle was supposed to have been built by Alan, son of Flaad, to whom William the Conqueror gave the manor. A circular bailey with water in the ditch below the mound and a few pieces of masonry lie there.

The Norman keep is depicted on the Sign together with a soldier of that period, and on the post below is a replica of the sword found in the village (now preserved in the Castle Museum, Norwich).

The Sign is situated where, in the past, the poor could obtain free coal, and the base is constructed from flints taken from the old coal house. This is another example of Mr. Harry Carter's work and was erected in October 1973.

Mrs. Mellows and Mrs. Starling collected £130 to cover the cost.

NEAR MILEHAM CHURCH

MILEHAM

MUNDESLEY

Mundesley is a small seaside resort about five miles from Cromer. It has steep sandy cliffs, a wide beach. and extensive views of the sea. With its safe bathing facilities it grew in popularity in the early C19, at the time that its larger neighbour Cromer was gaining importance as a holiday centre, nevertheless, Mundesley has kept its own individuality to which it owes its great charm. In the season it never becomes very trippery or overcrowded. After which it reverts to its own quiet existence. Having sprung from the modest beginnings of a fishing village, it has merely become larger without becoming pretentious.

Looking at the village sign, you will see on it a picture showing an attractive scene of a seaside subject, captured and perpetuated for all to see it, of Mundesley as it was in the past, and as people living there now would like it to be remembered in the future, namely as a little North Norfolk fishing village. So a typical old part is shown — a slipway and the Lifeboat Inn and an old boat such as the fishermen still use, when they row out to their crabpots for the celebrated "Cromer Crabs" — a great Norfolk delicacy. The scene is all very true to life, and therefore very pleasing. This delightful sign stands in High Street, in a very pretty garden setting.

It was a gift from the Carter family, in memory of Mrs. Alice Carter. It was made by Mr. Harry Carter, who is to be numbered amongst this well known local family.

And so the sign does two things, it recalls to mind Mundesley in its very early days, and a much loved person. No happier memorial could have been raised!

MUNDESLEY

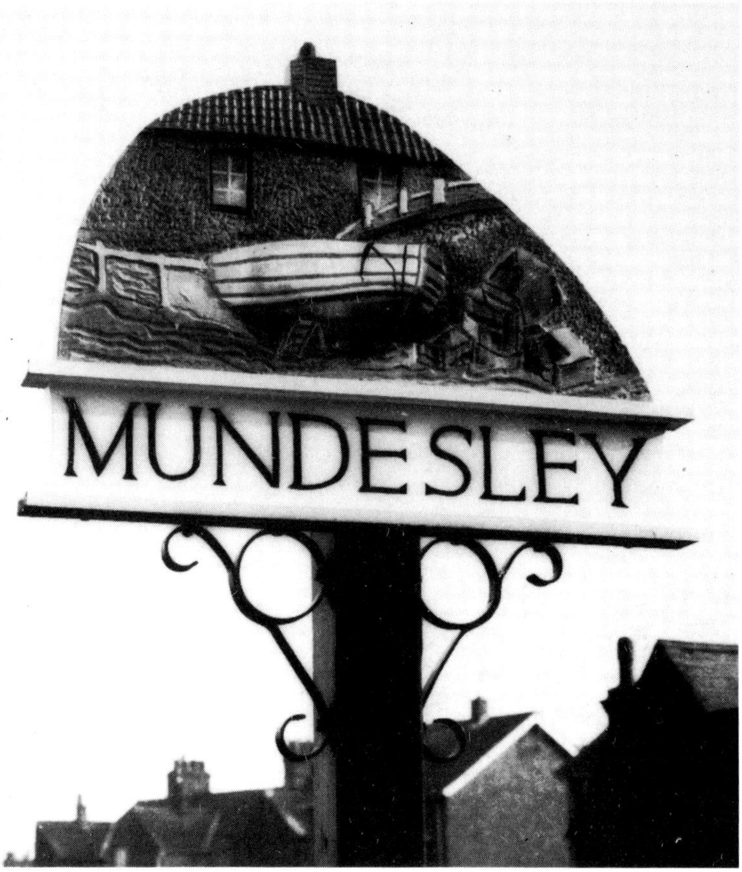
MUNDESLEY

MUNDFORD

Mundford is an ancient village and is mentioned in Domesday Book. It is near the river Wissey, on the border of Thetford Chase. It is fairly large, and full of character with its houses built in the style that betokens its Breckland origin, for all this district is in the Breckland area, that great tract of heath, which, after centuries of being barren and unproductive, owing to its infertile soil, is now under the reafforestation scheme, so that you see miles of orderly ranks of shady trees, and is at long last reclaimed and becoming a valuable asset. One thing there was in plenty, and that was flint, and as houses built in flint will last longer than those constructed in other building materials, this accounts for the strong and permanent appearance of some of the dwellings, whilst many others are robust and Georgian in style.

One cannot fail to be impressed with the place, it is quiet and dignified, and decidedly pleasing. It has an interesting church and a charming green on which stands the village sign which was given by an anonymous donor, and made by Mr. Harry Carter. It shows a manor house of the C16 century, and outside it stand a man and woman dressed in costumes of the same period. The two figures represent two members of the de Mundford family which owned the estate. There is a similar picture on the other side.

The sign was unveiled by two "senior citizens", eighty nine year old Mr. Arthur Shinn, and eighty five year old Mrs. Mary Jarred, both looking so full of good health and good spirits as to recommend Mundford as a second Shangri-La!

MUNDFORD

MUNDFORD

NEATISHEAD

We become very accustomed to seeing the pictorial type of sign, so much so that when we are confronted with one that consists of coats of arms, we may, if we know nothing of heraldry, feel puzzled and at a loss to interpret it. However with some explanatory help, they can be most informative. Take for example the sign in the very attractive little village of Neatishead, which is both interesting and well designed; and under which there is a small plaque which tells very clearly, the meaning of the three different shields on it. (How very thoughtful of the signmakers to help us in this way). On very few signs is there any explanation given, and yet without such help, the meaning is not properly understood by the visitors who have probably no knowledge of local history. Future sign makers would do well to remember that many people come from far away, just to look at our signs, and miss much of the pleasure if they do not understand the meaning of what they are looking at.

With regard to the sign at Neatishead, in the centre is the shield of St. Benet's Abbey, now but a sad fragment of a ruin, which can be seen by many holiday makers on the Broads as they proceed down the river Bure. It was once a large and influential abbey, and after at length, it fell from power, through the despicable treachery of one of its own monks, the Bishop of Norwich became its abbot, in name only now, of course, for its abbey as such is but a ghost of its former self. But once a year, on the first Sunday in August, the bishop comes and holds a service, and preaches to the holiday makers who fill the river with their craft, and crowd on to the land around the ruins of the ancient gateway (within which there is the tower of a later ruined windmill) to take part in this unique occasion. It makes a memorable sight! On the left of the sign, is the coat of arms of the Preston family, who are the local land owners on whose land the village is built, and have held it since they acquired it in the C17. To the right is the badge of the Royal Air Force, who have built a radar station nearby. The

NEATISHEAD

name Nethershird at the top of the sign is the old spelling of its name from earliest times, and which was taken from a document dated AD 1082. This striking sign was designed by Mr. Roger Challinor, who together with Mr. Alan Brown painted it. The beautifully made iron work is from the anvil of Mr. Eric Stevenson, who you may remember made the exquisite iron work for the fine sign at Kenninghall. The post and base were made by the local builders Harvey and Colk. The villagers who contributed to the cost of the sign may feel justifiably proud of it, for it is well worked out in every detail.

OUTWELL

Outwell is a town divided lengthwise by its river called Well Creek. It is mainly in Norfolk but partly in Cambridgeshire, and winds its way for two or three miles facing Upwell on its western side. It has a fine church built of warm coloured stone and several bridges, but the two features of particular interest are shown on the double sided Village Sign, standing in splendid isolation on the roadside verge. It was erected in 1977 to commemorate the Silver Jubilee of Queen Elizabeth II.

On the north side we are reminded of the once important Beaupré Hall which takes its name from the family who acquired lands here in the time of Edward VI. There is a 16th century tomb to Edmunde and Nicholas de Beaupré in the church. The property then passed to the Bells, one of whom married Sir Henry Hobart of Blickling Hall, and you can see his arms quartered with hers above the porch there. Later, by marriage, the Townley family came to Beaupré Hall and the Reverend W. G. Townley built the handsome suspension bridge at Welney in 1826.

Beaupré Hall was a brick mansion, its facade dated 1525, and possessed a gatehouse with turrets as shown on the sign.

On the south side is depicted Well Creek which is Outwell's special claim to fame, and almost unique it is too! For the navigable creek is carried by Mullicourt aqueduct across and **over** the great drain known as Middle Level. A laden barge comes towards us, possibly carrying produce from this area to Wisbech and onto Lynn, for this is a very fertile area of silty fen, with many smallholdings, encouraging the production of great quantities of strawberries and other fruit, as well as potatoes and flowers.

In winter it is often possible — as it is at Welney — to indulge in speed skating, a very popular sport, along the winding ways of Well Creek.

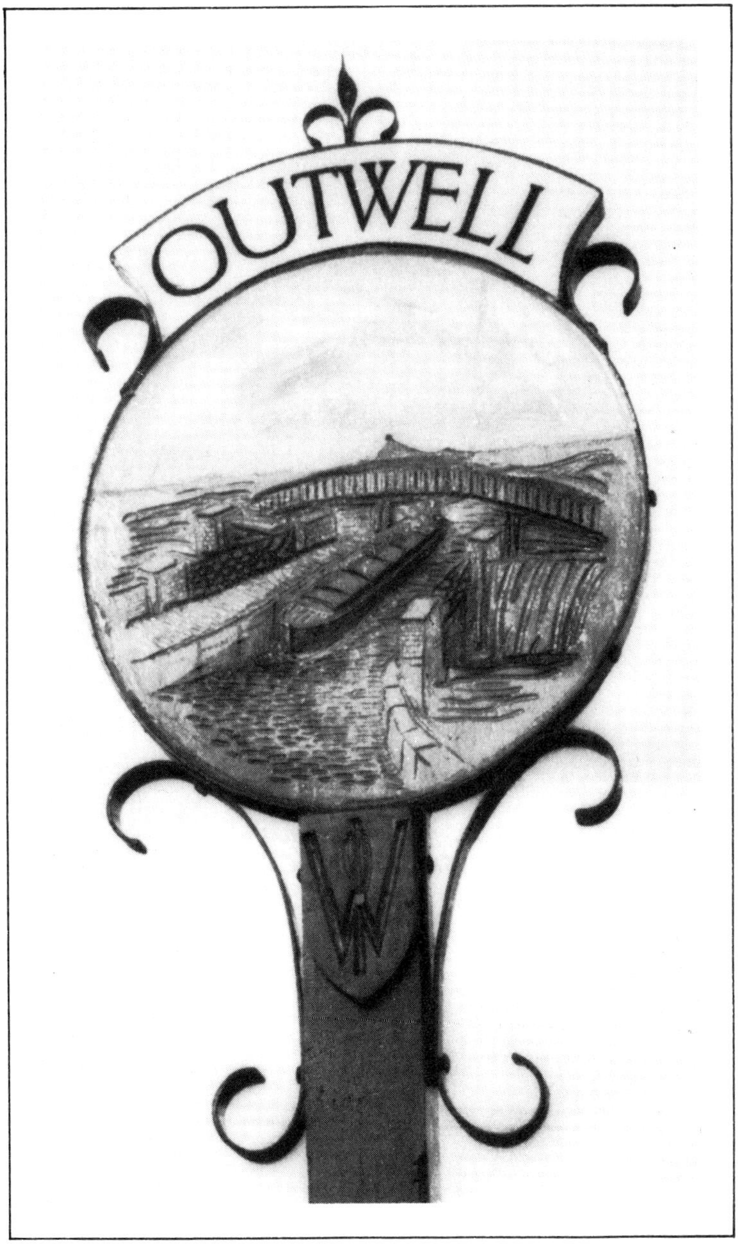
OUTWELL

OVERSTRAND

Overstrand is situated on the coast two miles south-east of Cromer. It has a fine beach, bracing air, and although much appreciated by holiday makers, it is still largely a residential place, with attractive houses and pleasant gardens.

As is not uncommon anywhere along the East Anglian coast, shipwrecks occur from time to time, and in the remote past it was also much subjected to Viking raids, whilst several generations ago smugglers found the coastline very suitable for their activities, the sandy beaches being very accessible for landing their shallow bottomed boats. But the greatest menace of all has been the ever encroaching sea, which pounding relentlessly against the soft sandy cliffs, has eroded the coastline extensively despite the efforts to protect it.

The village sign contains references to all these facts, and you will probably derive much interest in observing the way they are all incorporated in it.

On the front of the sign is depicted a shipwreck from which a man has fortunately escaped, and as he scrambled ashore he is met by a woman named Rebecca Hythe, who at one time, it is **said,** kept an inn on the top of the cliff, which has long since fallen into the sea, and in its time was popular with sailors and smugglers. In "White's Directory of Norfolk" of 1845, it is recorded that on the beach there was a fishing station called Beck Hythe, where there were curing houses, and some fishing boats were moored. Surely this is a strange co-incidence?

On the reverse side two men — a Dane and a Saxon — stand in front of a ruined ecclesiastical building. The men represent the long struggle when the Vikings were frequently attacking the hapless Saxons in this region. The ruined building bears witness to the ancient church, which in 1398 fell into the sea. (The first of three churches built here.) A large black dog is seen too. This is a legendary creature (probably derived from Viking mythology) named Black Shuck, which is said to haunt the East Anglian coast from end to end. To see him is a sign of ill-omen, even a presage of death! He is generally to be seen tearing along, with wildly glaring eyes — or even headless! Belief in this terrifying creature dies hard, and there are written testimonies as evidence, from people of undoubted integrity, who witnessed seeing him personally. Believe it or not, but **hope not** to see him! Finally the man on horseback represents a smuggler; the crab reminds us of the excellent Cromer crabs, much in favour, and still plentiful, also a man with his crab pots stands by the sea wall. The poppy recalls the name given to this district on account of great drifts of poppies which added brilliant colouring to this attractive Norfolk landscape and which became known as "Poppyland", after the publication of the romantic and popular song by Clement Scott, called "The Garden of Sleep".

This delightful sign was made by Mr. Harry Carter, and stands on a suitable and well constructed base made by Mr. John Worthington — a local resident. It was erected by the Overstrand Women's Institute to commemorate the Queen's Silver Jubilee.

PALLING
(Also known as Sea Palling)

Without doubt this is the most dramatic sign up to date. There are now more than 250 signs in Norfolk, and they tell of historical events, and personages, old customs, fables and legends, religious houses, witchcraft and fairs, or refer to our great agricultural heritage throughout the ages; Romans, Saxons and Normans figure in them; watermills and windmills appear; wherries and other craft abound. What a variety! Except for fishing, wildfowl and smugglers, it seems to be forgotten that we have a coastline — both in the north and down our eastern borders. Yet there is only one mention of the Lifeboat Institution, despite innumerable heroic rescues from raging, perilous seas. The one exception is at Caister-on-Sea where it shows a spirited but formalised lifeboat on one side of its sign.

It cannot be appreciated enough, except in Norfolk, that the coastline is bare of natural harbours, and that our shores are at the mercy of the wild North Sea, and that violent and sudden storms seem to come up suddenly out of nowhere, with great violence and relentless fury, making rescues most dangerous and hazardous. And yet there are many lifeboats in service, and deeds of incredible bravery are not infrequent. But at last one place has produced a sign where a lifeboat is not merely included, but shown in action with startling reality, and that is here at Palling, where they still have a lifeboat. This small informal seaside place has magnificent views of the sea, with a wild coastline of sand and shingle, backed with sandhills of rough marram grass. It would be difficult enough to portray a lifeboat in action on a large canvas, but it must be realised that a village sign is generally limited to about one yard wide, or thereabouts, in which to convey a moment of great stress and drama, of a small boat on a merciless sea at the terrifying moment when the vessel is on the crest of a precipitous wave and about to plunge into a deep chasm of dark waters, in imminent danger of capsizing and which brave men must face again and again to save the helpless victims of shipwreck. The crew are all volunteers, mostly hard working seafaring men — and

SEA PALLING

others — from modest homes, who risk their lives time without number in the service of their fellow-creatures in the interests of humanity. And it is only of recent years that lifeboats are machine propelled, and not man powered. Mr. Harry Carter has carved this remarkably fine sign from an original design by Mr. Henry Barnett, of Palling, and it should rank amongst one of his most successful achievements.

The emblems below the main theme are easy to interpret. The fish refer to the fishing, the corn to the farming hereabouts, and the key indicates that the parish church was dedicated to the great fisherman St. Peter. The carved fish brackets are also very beautifully portrayed. The sign was provided by the Sea Palling and Waxham Residents' Association, whose chairman, Mr. Thomas Lowell introduced Mr. Percy Feek who unveiled it. This was a most appropriate choice as Mr. Feek was one of the old lifeboat crew.

Lastly, the Palling lifeboat has, in its time, saved no less than 787 lives, which is surely a most remarkable record?

PASTON

Although Paston is only a small hamlet on the main coast road from Bacton to Mundesley, most of the dwellings lie beyond the Church and Hall, beside which stands a huge barn preventing the road from maintaining its course without a distinct kink. The name of Paston is famous as the original home of that great family of prominent lawyers and statesmen who took their name from the village, and from whom came the series of letters so fortunately preserved, which provide such a fascinating picture of life in the 15th century.

The Village Sign which was erected in 1953 to commemorate the Coronation of Queen Elizabeth II was, and is in 1978, the only swinging one; recently it has been moved to the opposite side of the road and has been repainted. It shows the arms of the Paston family and a scroll and quill to remind us of the famous letters. The magnificent barn built by William Paston in 1581 and the cornmill on the hill leading down to Mundesley can be seen today and are both illustrated on the Sign.

PASTON

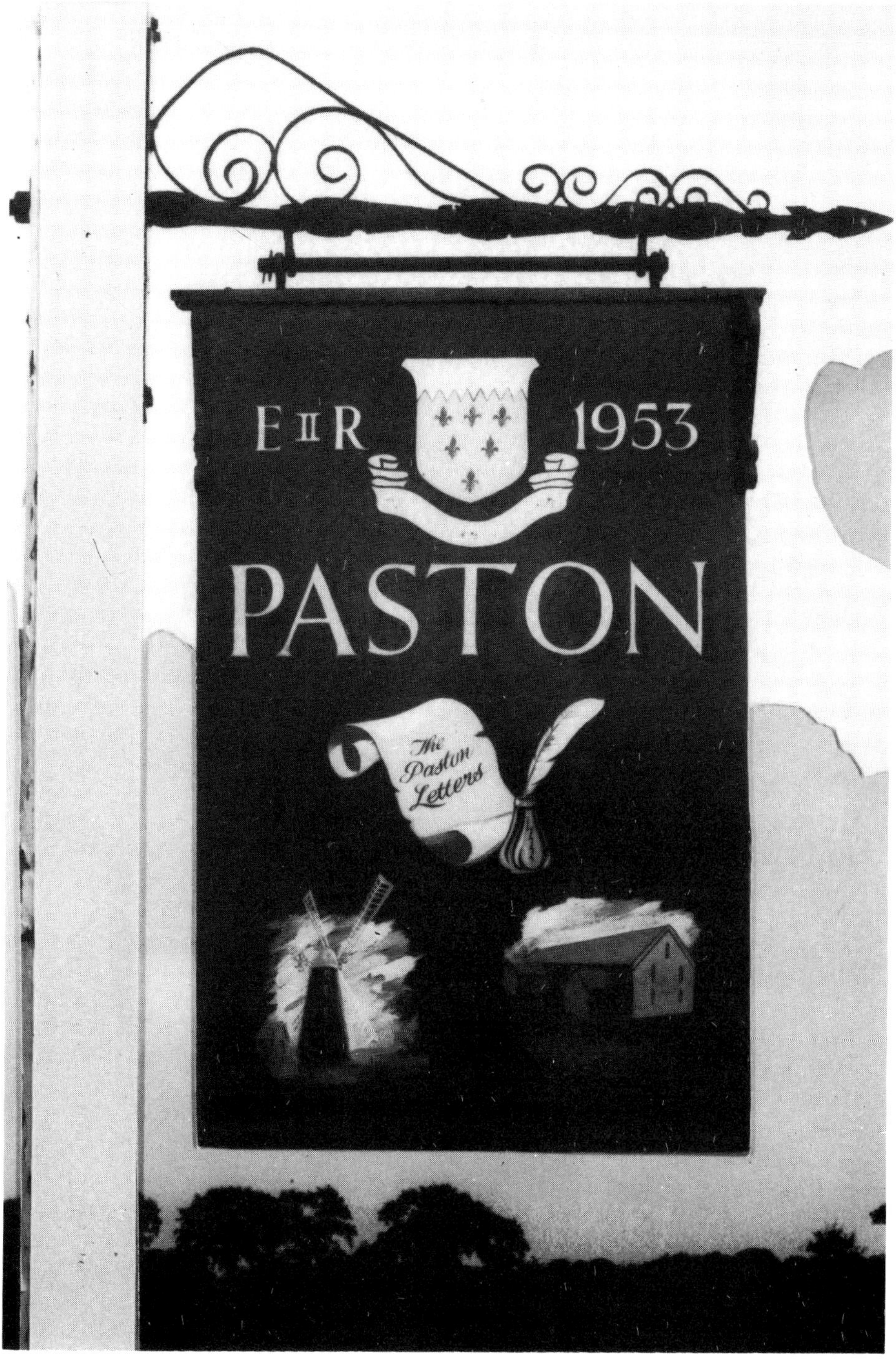
E II R
1953
PASTON
The Paston Letters

PENTNEY

    Pentney is situated in the valley of the Nar, and lies about one mile west of Narborough. The name is derived from the Old English and means "Penta's Island or waterlands" — which clearly described its nature. It was here that Robert Vallibus (sometimes mentioned as Vaux) held the manor from Roger Bigod and founded a priory in the C12 for Augustinian Canons. This community of fifteen to twenty men were not monks, but priests, whose purpose was — in brief— to instruct and teach church doctrine according to the traditions of St. Augustine. This was always a well conducted community with an excellent reputation. It lasted until the Dissolution of the Monasteries in the reign of King Henry VIII. There are now only slight remains of this great priory, except for the magnificent gateway. It is built in flint, has two storeys, and battlements, and on either side it is flanked with turrets and is a most impressive sight. It is about 1½ miles from the parish church. The sign was erected to celebrate the Queen's Silver Jubilee, and was carved and painted by "Mr. Zed", who has made, amongst others, the sign at East Rudham. This sign at Pentney is also beautifully designed and made. It bears on its central panel a striking representation of the Priory Gatehouse. Below it is shown a barge which represents the typical river borne transport of such commodities as corn and other cereals, coal and vegetables, which were conveyed frequently along the river Nar, to and from the port of King's Lynn. It is of interest to note that in the C19 the whole village was officially drained — which must have made the soil considerably more productive, and the whole area healthier and pleasanter in which to live.

PENTNEY

PENTNEY

POTTER HEIGHAM

Norfolk is unique for its wide variety of Village Signs, each telling a story of history or legend relative to that particular area. Some seem to have little to record while others like Potter Heigham can contribute a wealth of interesting detail. Here the people have even included relevant notes on two plaques fastened to the flint base. The Sign is double-sided, which provides plenty of scope for portraying any facts.

The scene on the top of the Sign shows the old 15th century arched bridge which is still used, especially by holiday makers arriving in their cars to this busy boating centre on the Norfolk Broads. The arches are so small, even the middle one, that an experienced pilot is essential when boats wish to pass beneath. Vast areas of huge sheds, to house and repair the fleets of cruisers, and the many inlets and quays surrounding them, can be seen from this bridge. The Village Sign is nearby, although the village proper is some half-mile away and across the new motor road.

The south side of the Sign shows a horse and cart being driven over the bridge while a trading wherry is lying at the quay below, its cargo of reeds is being unloaded — reeds cut from the many acres of reed-beds around the Broads of Hickling and Horsey. Norfolk reeds are said to be the finest in the country.

The vertical panel and the spandrels are concerned with the Romans, whose craft of making pottery was carried on here, in this case urns are being made to contain the ashes of the dead, all recorded in rich colours by Mr. Harry Carter. The original site of Pot Hills can be seen in the north-east of the parish and the industry is perpetuated in the village name. Heigham is of Saxon origin meaning town.

POTTER HEIGHAM

On the other side of the Sign (and the bridge), the cart or waggon and its loads are more easily seen and two men are busy below. In the vertical panel there is a typically modern view of sailing and motor boats, a fisherman and a bird-watcher in his "hide" on a bright and breezy day. Below this is a peat digger and piles of neatly cut turf, recalling medieval times when peat was used for fuel, as most timber had been felled. Later it was these "diggings" which, becoming flooded, formed the Broads as we know them today — in other words, broad shallow lakes which are connected to the five main rivers.

In the spandrels above are seen the Heron and the Bittern, two large and shy birds which still thrive in the district despite the turmoil of the 20th century.

The Sign was erected in 1975.

PULHAM ST. MARY

There are two Pulhams, Pulham St. Mary and Pulham Market, a few miles north west of Harleston

Pulham St. Mary is a pleasant place with a fine church, and in the village centre is a double-sided sign of absolute simplicity, a straight-forward and no-nonsense picture recalling an outstanding episode in Pulham's past.

An airship, the R 33, sometimes jokingly called "the Pulham Pig", is tethered to its mooring mast against a clear sky except for the great clouds overhead, symbolic perhaps ? of the disasters hanging over the fate of such vast dirigibles in the era before the second world war.

It was as far back as 1852 that controlled flight in an airship was attempted, but it was 1884 before a successful one was launched in France. Other countries experimented and it was a Count Zeppelin who succeeded in 1908, and whose name was given to those enormous German airships which were only too familiar to some of our senior citizens in the Great War.

In 1929 the Graf Zeppelin was flown round the world in twenty-one days. In Britain the R 33 and its sister ship R 34 were built in vast hangars near the railway at Pulham. The R 34 flew successfully from England to America and back (1919). Both airships were based on the design of a German one captured in 1916.

On August 16 1925 there arose a great gale and the R33 was straining at her mooring mast and awaiting trials.

PULHAM ST MARY

The new crew, two members of the R.A.F. and eighteen civilians had just come aboard. About two hours later the mooring arm snapped and the R 33's nose was badly crushed, (some sixty feet of this 640 foot long airship,) then in hurricane force winds the whole airship broke away. The engines were started but such was the gale that nothing could stop the steady drift towards the Continent. Luckily they were well equipped with fuel and food. Trying to steer a northerly course round the storm proved impossible and the R 33 almost reached Holland. During the night however the drift was checked and the crew and passengers were no doubt more than thankful to arrive back in England shortly before 3.20 pm.

Five years later the loss of Britain's 101, and an American airship in 1933, caused the authorities in many countries to abandon further construction. However in 1979 there has been talk of a new and safer type of airship in the pipeline.

The idea for the Village Sign was suggested by Mr. Wilfred Wharton and was carved and painted by Mr. Wing, a sign-writer of note. Funds were raised through donations and various communal efforts and the sign was to celebrate the Queen's Jubilee in 1977. It was put up on the day of the Thanksgiving Service.

QUIDENHAM

Quidenham parish has been almost entirely owned by the Earls of Albemarle for over two centuries. The family seat was Quidenham Hall until, in 1948, it was turned into a convent for Carmelite nuns.

The village is small and remote, set in the midst of wooded country. A mile-long avenue leads past the Hall entrance towards a mound where legend tells us that it was the grave of Boadicea, the famous warrior Queen of the Iceni tribe, who held her court nearby at Kenninghall and was the inspiration for the Village Sign designed by Mrs. P. MacNamara (who was also responsible for the very fine one at Kenninghall). It has been carried out in painted metal.

The Sign is well sited beside the road with a clear view across the village green, and shows Boadicea, or more correctly Boudicca, in her chariot, driving her spirited horses with all the verve expected of such a leader.

QUIDENHAM

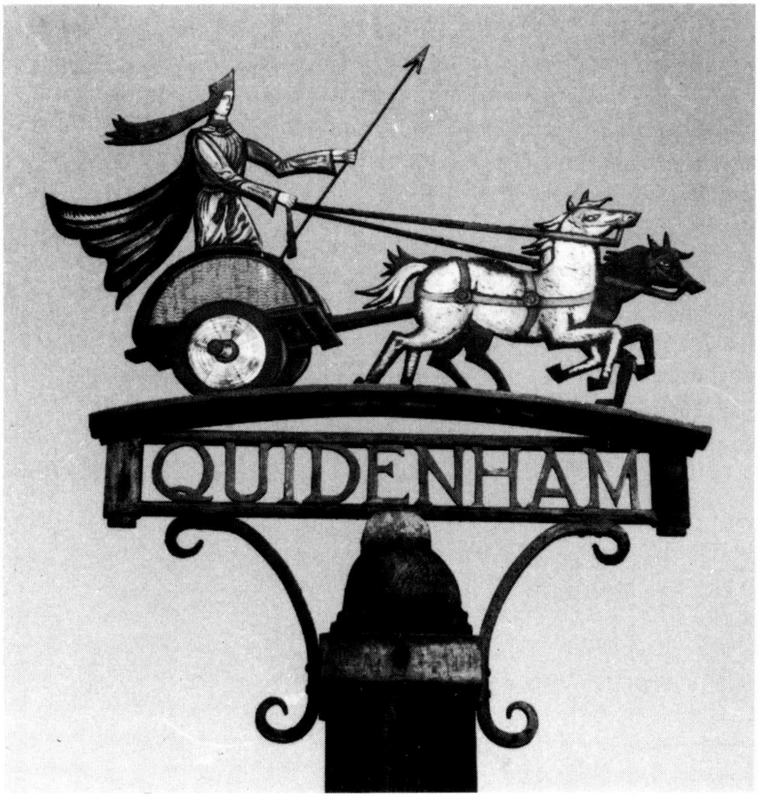
QUIDENHAM

RAVENINGHAM

Raveningham is a village of scattered houses, set in pretty, peaceful country, about 7-8 miles south-east of Norwich; there is not much evidence of change, and it is much as it has been for many a long year. In a lovely parkland of fine, old trees, stands Raveningham Hall, the home of the Bacon family. It is a dignified Georgian mansion, mellowed with age, with a homely lived-in look about it. The Bacons have been connected with Norfolk for centuries, and are descended from the same Bacons who were so important in the reign of Queen Elizabeth I, especially Sir Nicholas Bacon, the Keeper of the Great Seal. In the church are many memorials to them. And there are memorials too, to the Castells (or Castylles), including a brass portraying Margaret Castylle, with a dragon at her feet, whilst in the folds of her gown lies a little dog with bells on his collar. As you might expect, at some time the two families became united by marriage.

The name Raveningham originally meant "the home of Hraefn's people". and the pronunciation of Hraefn has become "raven", — thus — the village sign is partly a rebus, for the raven represents the beginning of the name of the place. The castle is to bring to your mind the Castell family, and the significance of the moat is because you can still find the old moated manor house, which stands in the village, and is now a farm.

This original and excellent village sign incorporates much of the relevant past of this quiet, secluded village.

Mr. Joe Pye, a gamekeeper, who lives on the estate, made the sign, which clearly shows that he has a flair for such things! He made it of local wood given by the Lord of the Manor, Sir Edmund Bacon, who is also the premier Baronet of England. When it was erected there were celebrations at the hall, which were even described as a "feast"; — and the artist was not paid in the usual way but was presented with a purse containing contributions from grateful and appreciative parishioners.

This village sign is full of interest, and on it are so many references to items of local significance that it has a crowded appearance, enough to make one wonder how one place could have so much to impart. But with a little explanation one feels that this small, pretty village has not been without many interesting events in its past.

The sign stands on a steep little bank, where a road forks, and at first when erected, seemed rather too high to photograph advantageously. But since then the site has been improved, and now several well-placed steps have made it easier to approach, and enhanced its appearance considerably. It would be better still if those responsible for its erection would do as they have done at Potter Heigham and several other places, and put below it some clear, and helpful information, thus making it easier for the uninitiated to understand it. However for your better appreciation of this sign, here are some very brief notes to enlighten you. There are eleven symbols to see in the carvings, and these are a record of historical, social and natural associations of the parish and people connected with them.

(1) The church tower represents the parish church, dedicated to St. Mary the Virgin. (2) The left hand shield bears one of her symbols, a reference to the words of St. Simeon, "A sword shall pierce through your own heart also". (3) The other shield is that of St. Benet's Abbey, because William Ruggs (or Repps), was its last abbot before the dissolution. (4) The cittern, a lute-like instrument, informs us that John Playford, was born here in 1623, and wrote a book of lessons for this instrument. (5) The barrel and post refer to a smuggling incident concerning a chief preventive officer, named Hickman. (6) The open fetters refer to Sir Thomas Fowell-Buxton, a great advocate for the abolition of slavery, who lived at Northrepps Hall. (7) The Breeches-Buoy was first tested here, at

NORTH REPPS

Northrepps Hall, directed by Anna Gurney. (8) The radiator is that of the Rolls Royce Silver Ghost. Henry Royce developed this famous engine whilst living in this parish. (9) The "Gallas" plough, widely used until the 1920s was made at the local foundry here; another representation of it can also be seen in the church weather vane. (10) The Thornhill railway bridge draws attention to the fact that there are seventeen such bridges in this parish. (11) The poppy still flourishes in the cornfields, and remind you that you are in the region of "Poppyland".

The sign was designed and painted by Mr. David Ainsworth; it was carved by Mr. Derek Gardner. It was built by Mr. John Golden, and the joiner was Mr. William Pardon.

You will find this sign full of interest and variety; and you will notice that commendable virtue, that it is a village sign in every sense of the word.

ROLLESBY

Rollesby, with its neighbouring villages of Filby and Ormesby, also has a broad of the same name, and all these names signify Danish influence, for in the past these Saxon settlements were much harassed and ravaged by the invading, and victorious Vikings, who for over two centuries were a perpetual menace to our shores. The sign at Rollesby, unlike Filby and Ormesby, bears no reference to its historical past, but instead emphasises its strong links with the age-old industry of farming, its importance being due to its continued rich harvests on which the ever increasing requirements of a growing population depends.

The farming industry is continually losing valuable agricultural land to the insatiable demand for space on which to build more houses and factories, and to the ever increasing construction of modern roads to bear the burden of lorries and enormous modern transport containers, which if it were not due to the closing of so many railways, might reasonably be expected to bear them instead. So the well designed and beautifully constructed sign at Rollesby takes the form of a plough.

There are quite a few villages in Norfolk, which, because of their association with agriculture have adopted a plough for their village sign; but note, if you will, the various ways in which they are presented, all of which have called for much ingenuity by the designer, craftsmen and artists responsible for them. This plough is not full sized, but is a scale model, and complete in every detail. It stands on the top of a sturdy name plate, with "E II R" carved on one end, and "Silver Jubilee" on the other. Below this is a device enclosing a cross, which represents the emblem of St. George, the patron saint of the ancient parish church.

The sign was paid for by public subscription. It was designed and made by two members of the staff of the Yarmouth College of Art — Mr. Geoffrey Buck and Mr. Jeremy Hough. The flint base was constructed by a local builder, Mr. Jacks.

This striking sign stands in an enclosed space, within the precincts of the village school grounds.

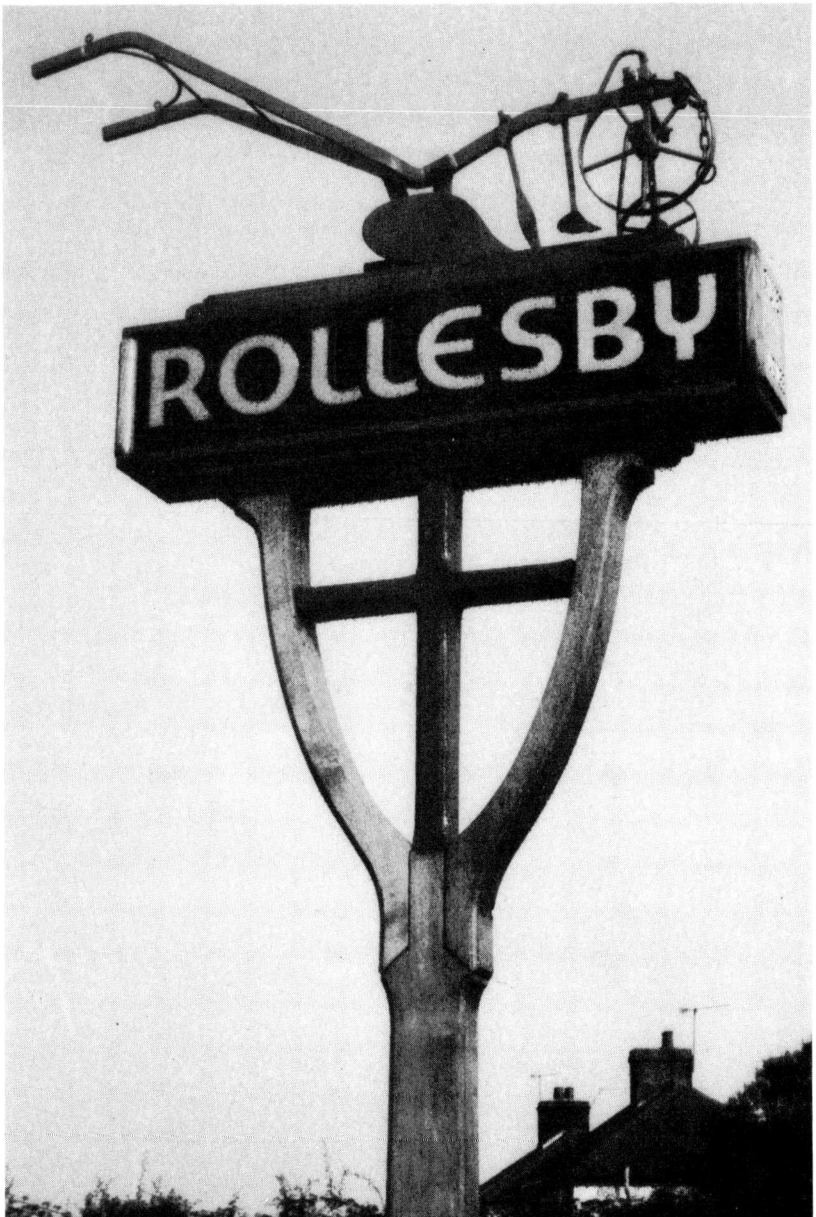
ROLLESBY

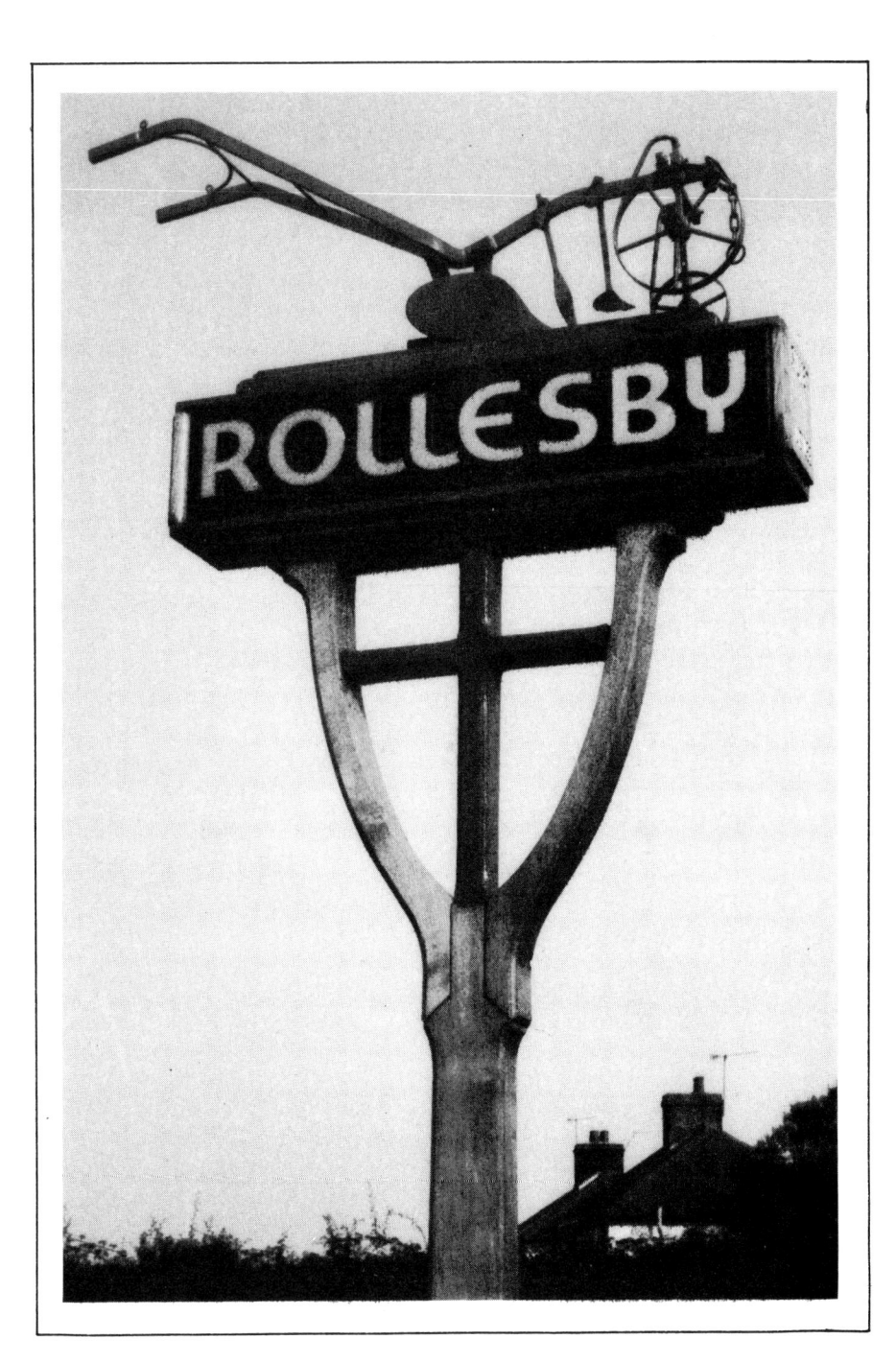

Roydon Church and the inn are on one side of the main road going west from Diss, and Roydon Hall on the other, all just over a mile from Bressingham, but most of the houses are along a loop road, north of the Hall, called Snow Street.

However, the Village Sign is to be seen almost opposite the church. Both Roydon and Bressingham signs were made by Mr. Harry Carter, for their joint Women's Institute group, whose varied and enthusiastic fund-raising activities produced the sum required.

On the Roydon sign we see a knight in armour standing before a rustic gateway, while above is a shield bearing two leopards' faces, and the whole is flanked by trees, of which there are many fine examples nearby. All this is to indicate the de Frere family, familiar in this district from the eleventh to the twentieth century!

Richard de Frere is said to have fought at the battle of Hastings, and Mrs. H. E. Frere was the first president of the local Women's Institute. One of the Freres, who were lords of the Manor, was John Hookham Frere who in the 19th century served in Parliament, was Spanish Ambassador, and was famous for his brilliant translations of the plays of Aristophanes. And another was Sir Henry Bartle Frere, who rendered invaluable service during his many years in India and who later became Governor of Cape Colony and an expert on South African affairs. There are several monuments to other members of the family in the church.

ROYDON

ROYDON

EAST RUDHAM

East Rudham has one of the most inspired signs in Norfolk, for it has as its subject the very moving experience of going on a pilgrimage to one of the greatest shrines in all Europe. It was designed and painted by one of our talented craftsmen — Mr. Stanley Zdziebczok, whose name will probably suggest to you — correctly — that he comes from Poland. He has an English wife, and he came to England over thirty years ago. Nevertheless he derived his skill and training from his native country being especially influenced by the carvings in its baroque churches; so it is not surprising that he approaches his work with devotion and reverence; in particular with regard to the story of Walsingham's shrine, and how it came to be built.

In the year 1061, Our Lady appeared to Richeldis, and showed her, in a vision, the house which stood before the cave of the Annunciation, and commanded her to build a replica in honour of Our Lord's Incarnation. The spot where it was to be built was shown by a spring of water which is known as "Our Lady's Well", the water of which has been used from that time for healing the sick from all kinds of disease and illness. This shrine is known as "England's Nazareth", and from then onwards attracted countless pilgrims from all over Europe for many years. From the time of Richard Coeur de Lion, until the reign of Henry VIII, nearly every king of England made pilgrimage to the "Holy House", including pilgrims from all over Europe, and both Augustinian Canons and Franciscan Friars cared for them, and ministered to their needs. But at the Reformation, this and other religious houses and shrines were demolished, their lands seized, their wealth confiscated, and their statues destroyed. For centuries Walsingham was neglected and forgotten, but rather more than fifty years ago it sprang into new life; its shrine has been rebuilt, before which candles burn again, services are resumed, and pilgrims come as before in ever increasing numbers to worship there.

In olden times pilgrims coming from the north, passed through East Rudham on their way to Walsingham to visit the shrine, and here on the Village Sign this is all so beautifully and reverently portrayed that it cannot fail to arouse appreciation and pleasure.

Below the scene showing the pilgrims on their way to Walsingham is another one, within a semicircle, of a ploughing theme which reminds us how dependent the village has always been on its agriculture. The shields below are of local interest too, referring to crops and woodland, and depicting East Rudham itself.

East Rudham

The village is most dignified, having an air of withdrawal and aloofness, as though turning away from the enormous amount of heavy commercial vehicles which pass through it in the direction of King's Lynn. The long narrow green looks an oasis of quiet, and its sign glows with colour, compelling attention.

The sign was given by Mr. H. Shephard in memory of his beloved wife.

One cannot think of a greater tribute to a well loved partner. The sign was unveiled as part of the Silver Jubilee Celebrations.

WEST RUNTON

West Runton lies between Cromer and Sheringham, an attractive, bracing, seaside place, but much smaller and less sophisticated. It is backed by sloping woods through which one sees delightful glimpses of the sea. As you follow the track, down which a glacial river once carved its way before shedding its load into the sea, and then cross the coast road, you will, before long, find yourself looking down from high sandy cliffs on to a fine beach, strewn in part with large flints, from which the sea never recedes far, and on to which it breaks in an eternal ballet of fascinating and rapidly changing wave patterns.

The village sign is situated on a green on the main coast road. In a semi-circular panel it bears a composite picture of West Runton's past features. On a hillside is a flock of sheep which belonged to the village, and down the post of the sign is carved a shepherd's crook: the fleeces would be valuable for their wool, and the animals would provide food for the community. The building is a brick kiln which was at Oxwell Cross on the coast road until it was demolished in 1951.

The hill called Incleborough Hill, shown on old maps, has been described as the highest free standing hill in the county and it is now covered by the well-known golf links. Finally, on the picture, the sea with a boat on it is to be observed in the distance.

Below the sign are emblems which indicate that the sign was a gift of the local Women's Institute, and that it was erected in the year of the Queen's Silver Jubilee. The sign was made by Mr. Harry Carter, and funds were sufficient to allow for a strong wooden seat to be placed near it.

Miss J. M. Moore provided for the cost of the base in memory of her sister, and Mr. W. J. Massingham constructed it.

This is the sign about which Mr. Ian Wallace said, on unveiling it — that village signs are an expression of pride on the part of the village as well as an expression of welcome. Never were words more aptly spoken in describing the purpose of a village sign!

WEST RUNTON

WEST RUNTON

ER 1977

RUSHALL

Rushall is a small village set in a landscape of wide farming country. Like many another, it has always been connected with agriculture, and that is the theme of its village sign.

One would suppose that with so many villages referring to their dependence on farming that they must needs fall back on a variation of the plough to indicate their way of life; but the Rushall people have thought of another important aspect of agriculture with which to draw attention to their occupation on the land; original and most interesting and pleasing — the culmination of the farming year!

Entering the village where three roads meet, one sees on a tiny triangle of grass, a firm brick base on which the sign is mounted. This is cut out of sheet metal similar to an iron sign, with the exception that this is an alloy, and as the light falls on it, it gleams like gold — an exhilarating sight. And thus the farming motif presents an inspiring aspect — the time of glorious achievement, when hopes are fulfilled, and the golden grain is harvested.

The machine is not the large, complex, and rather overpowering giant of efficiency of our later days, but one which was a common sight not long ago — the "sail-binder", which it must be admitted is more picturesque than the combine-harvester, however much it may be the farmer's idea of perfection!

The sign was erected in the year of the Queen's Silver Jubilee, by a small community which has at last achieved its great ambition, and is what so many villages hope ultimately to attain — a sign of their own! What a splendid thing it will be when every village in Norfolk has one. The cost was borne by all the villagers, by what must have been a prodigious effort, for not only did they raise sufficient funds for that, but also for festivities on the great occasion, an oak notice board for the church, and a silver birch tree to be beside the coronation copper beech. The sign is mounted on an oak post reputed to be 500 years old; and the base was built by local craftsmen.

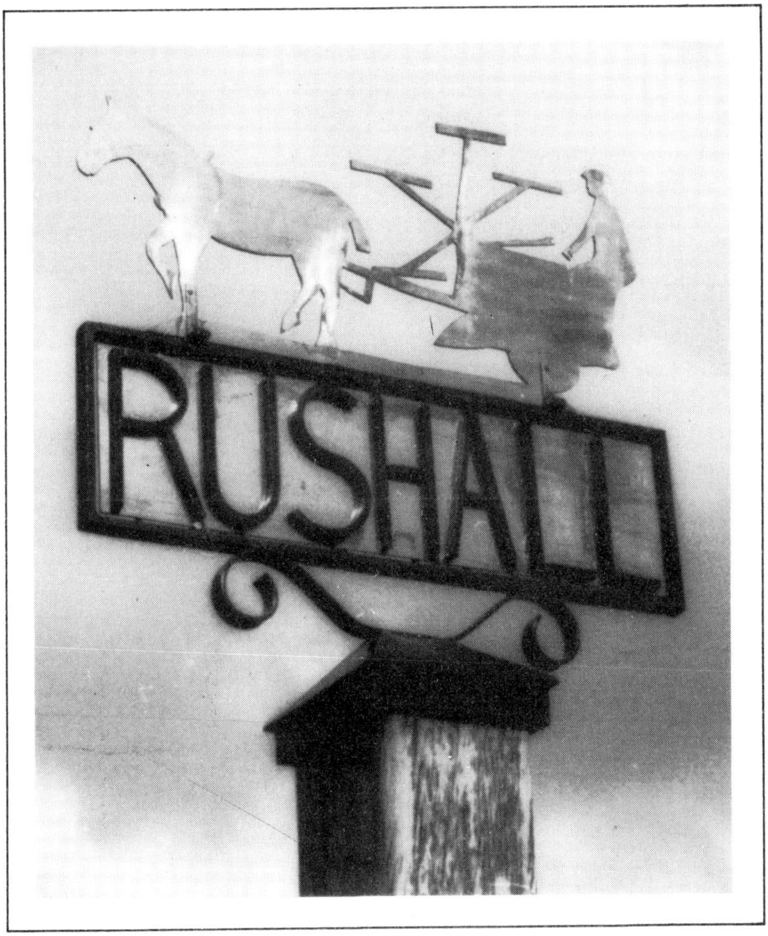
RUSHALL

GREAT RYBURGH

The approach to Great Ryburgh from the Guist — Fakenham road is quite delightful, going through quiet meadows towards a bridge, with a view of the Church of St. Andrew among the trees and across the clear waters of the river Wensum. Then after abrupt turns right and left one comes to the village, lining a street crossed centrally by the railway line. Not far from it is the semicircular Village Sign on its post, on which two scenes from the past are depicted.

On one side is shown the old maltings with a quantity of grain being unloaded while the horse waits patiently between the shafts of the waggon. Corn must also have been carted regularly to the watermill, which sadly now is completely derelict, but can be discovered at the other end of the village. On the other side of the Sign is pictured an old time fair, or Gant as it was called, the last of which took place about 1902. It was the custom, as this was held in May, to sell there gooseberry pies, a speciality of Great Ryburgh. To mark the unveiling of the sign, and the Golden Jubilee of the Women's Institute, two large gooseberry pies were baked by the President and a fellow-member for the great occasion.

The Sign was erected in May 1976, and donations came from various sources and local functions. It was again the work of Mr. Harry Carter.

GREAT RYBURGH

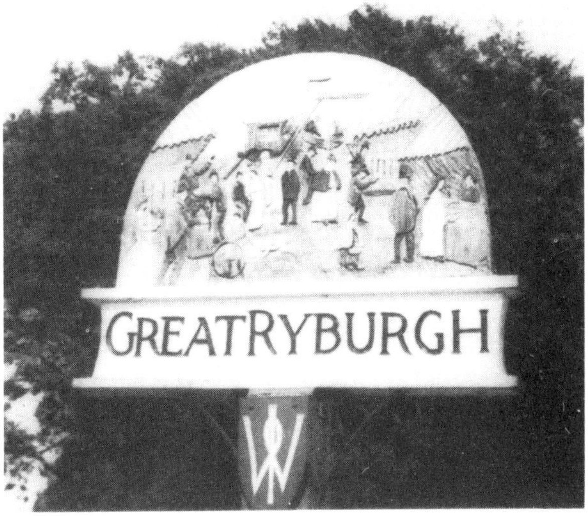
GREATRYBURGH

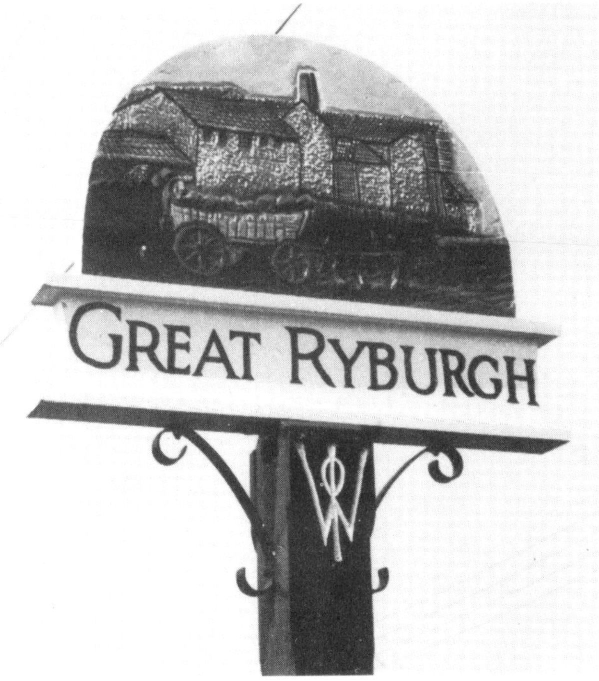
GREAT RYBURGH

SCOLE

Scole has grown up in four directions where the road from Diss to Yarmouth crosses the main road from Norwich to Ipswich, which was once a Roman highway down which their legions marched from Colchester to Venta Icenorum, the Roman station some three miles from Norwich.

The site of this crossing has been a major staging post throughout the centuries, from the days when it possessed a temporary shelter (the meaning of "Scole") to the time when the famous and picturesque White Hart Inn was built in 1655 by John Peck, a Norwich merchant, and which is considered one of the finest coaching inns in the country. Charles II is said to have breakfasted there and once there was a magnificent iron sign which spanned the entire roadway, an intricate fantasy of figures, animals and other motifs in profusion.

One can well imagine the stage coaches approaching, and the outriders proclaiming their imminent arrival by long blasts upon their post horns, whereupon a great deal of excitement and bustle would ensue!

On the Village Sign, placed almost opposite this Scole Inn, you can see the golden head of the Roman eagle and crossed post horns, reminding us of those two aspects of Scole's historic past. Below the horns is the saltire of St. Andrew, patron saint of the church nearby.

To the left and right are the shields of the Cornwallis and Shelton families, who were Lords of the Manor and who held sway over the district for long periods at different times.

At least two members of the Cornwallis family were outstanding men in the 18th century, one became Governor of India and a Marquess, and the other an Admiral who commanded the Channel fleet. Of the Sheltons, who were at the height of their power in Tudor times and lived in the village of Shelton, more than one became High Sheriff of Norfolk.

SCOLE

The Sign was erected in November 1976 and was again the work of Mr. Harry Carter. It has a stepped base of brick and flint made by a local builder. The necessary funds were raised by public subscription and the design was based on ideas submitted by the parishioners. Including some from the children.

SCOTTOW

The Jubilee Fund raised by the parishioners of Scottow enabled them to have a grand celebration at the time of the unveiling of their two Village Signs, one at each end of the parish.

The design for these identical signs was suggested by Mr. James Shaw of Scottow Hall and the work was carried out by Mr. Andrews, an expert at working at farm machinery — mending tractors etc.

The whole design is constructed from the shaping and welding of pieces of iron rod to show the date of the Queen's Silver Jubilee and the name of the parish.

Scottow is a scattered village inhabited mainly by communities near the Church and Hall and another on the main road near the Three Horse Shoes Inn, while the area around is very much dominated by the proximity of the R.A.F. airfield at Coltishall. One sign can be found on the modern road from Buxton to the B road leading to North Walsham and the other on the dual carriageway from Tunstead.

ALL SAINTS - SCOTTOW

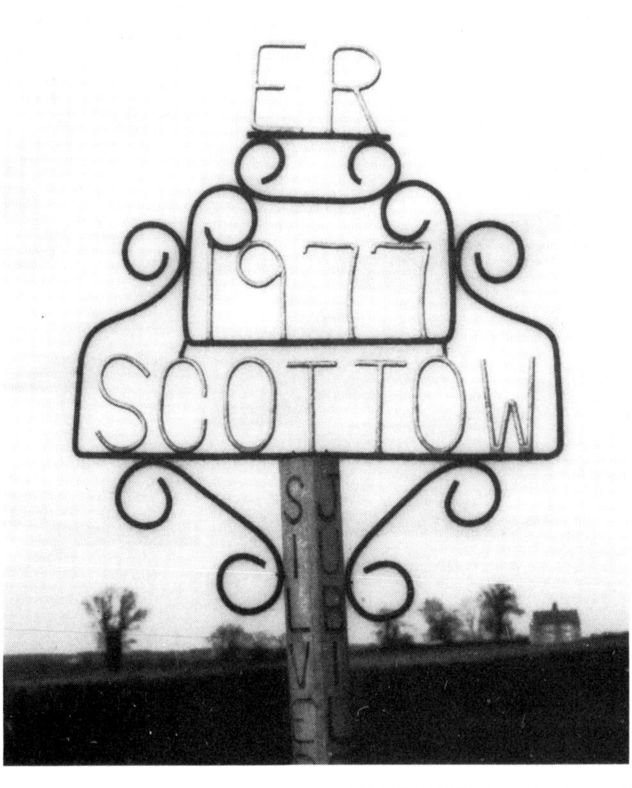
E R
1977
SCOTTOW

SHERINGHAM

Sheringham is one of the largest and most popular seaside resorts in Norfolk — and yet it is not too sophisticated — rather it a friendly little town, sheltered on the East and West by high cliffs and with many charming aspects of old Sheringham, and, of course, with plenty of crabpots in evidence! And yet when the summer season is over the town is not "dead" by any means; but because it is a thriving residential place it is full of interest and activity.

It has a town sign which in every way befits its dignity. Carved in Iroco wood it gives the impression of being made in bronze.

It was given by the Sheringham and District Chamber of Trade through donations from members of about £300. It stands outside the General Post Office in the town centre. The sign takes the form of a coat of arms, most beautifully carved by Mr. Joe Dawes of Saxthorpe from the design drawn up by Mr. Bob Lord who is an architectural designer. On the shield are two pine cones, and below them is a ship in full sail. This is to represent Sheringham as situated between woods and pine trees through which one passes when approaching the town, and the sea below. The helmet above, is surmounted by a lobster as a crest, and is indicative of the important fishing industry of the past, which is concentrated now on "Cromer crabs", for which this part of the coast is renowned — lobsters are not nearly so numerous as formerly, for reasons best known to the lobsters themselves apparently!

A rough rendering of the Latin inscription could read, "Both sea and pines adorn it" — which they most certainly do!

The base of the sign was provided by the Sheringham Development Company, and Mr. William Buddrell engraved the brass plate.

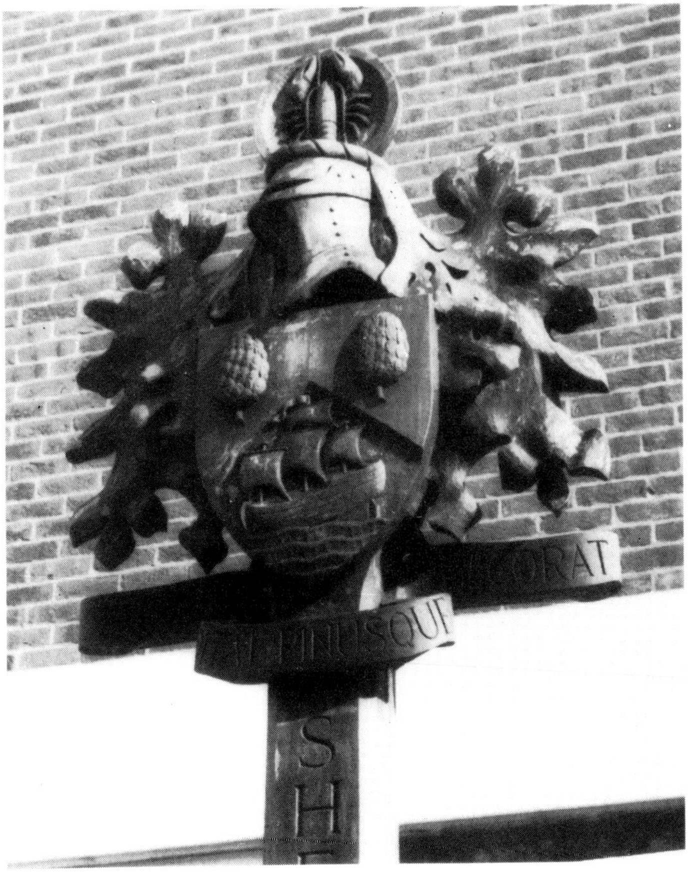
CORAT

SHOTESHAM

Shotesham lies in one of Norfolk's most delightful village settings of meadow and surrounding hills. The Church of All Saints stands sentinel at the end of the valley, high above the sweeping curve of road and attractive houses which confront the water meadows below.

The Village Sign, which has a coat of arms on one side and a priest-like figure on the other, not to mention an unusual type of conveyance on the top, calls attention to many interesting facts concerning the parish and others grouped with it.

There were once four churches (depicted on the four curved brackets) and in the Domesday survey this area was divided into twelve parts. The name Shotesham is derived from the Saxon word Scots, meaning Part. The figure in ecclesiastical robes represents St. Botolph, patron saint of one of the churches, who is supposed to have been an abbot in 655 A.D. The other two churches were SS Mary and Martin.

A brass plaque on the supporting posts tells of William Fellowes who founded here the first cottage hospital in England in 1771. Part of the original buildings now used as dwellings can be seen on the other side of the valley. Dr. Benjamin Gooch became the greatest English surgeon of his day and was in charge here. On account of the hospital's success it was moved to Norwich, where it is now known as the Norfolk and Norwich Hospital.

Shotesham Hall was built by Sir John Soane, a well-known architect, for William Fellowes. It is still the home, after two centuries, of the Fellowes family.

SHOTESHAM

The coat of arms on the Sign is that of the Mercers Company, the premier livery company of London, which became the trustees of the Earl of Northampton's Charity. Little Henry Howard was unexpectedly born here in the village in February 1539, as his mother was passing through in her carriage from Bungay Castle, naturally the Royal Party had to break its journey here. You can see them looking out on top of the Sign. Henry grew up to become a great and noble man, was made Earl of Northampton, yet remembered the poor of his birthplace.

GREAT SNORING

Great Snoring is a very attractive village, grouped around a junction of four roads on undulating ground, making a little centre, where the Village Sign stands, surrounded by picturesque creeper-clad houses, many of them built in the 18th century.

The Sign, presented by the local Women's Institute and made by Mr. Harry Carter, has a pleasing and different picture on each side. On one can be seen two horses ploughing, referring not only to the farming of the area but to the fact that agricultural machinery was made here. In the middle distance is the Church of St. Mary, and beyond that the old Rectory, once the manor house, renowned for its beautiful brickwork, and the former home of the Shelton family. There is also a representation of a windmill (a post mill) which, sadly, disappeared in the early 30's and which was situated on high ground to the south of the village.

On the reverse side of the Sign is pictured an even older mill, a watermill, of which there is mention in the Domesday Book in the 11th century. Scarcely any trace of it is left today, but it was obviously powered by the water in the upper reaches of, at this point, the little river Stiffkey, just beside the present bridge.

It seems that on both sides of this Sign Mr. Harry Carter has enjoyed the patterning of the surface, in the ripples in the river and the ridges on the ploughed field, and has succeeded most cleverly in getting a feeling of the freshness of the open countryside, even the effect of the blowing cloud shape adds to this. The Sign was completed in December 1976, and stands on Unicorn Knoll. Mr. Terry Hill was responsible for the base.

GREAT SNORING

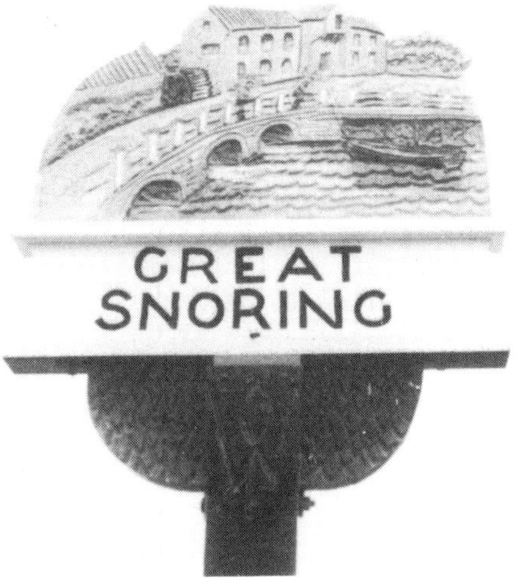
GREAT
SNORING

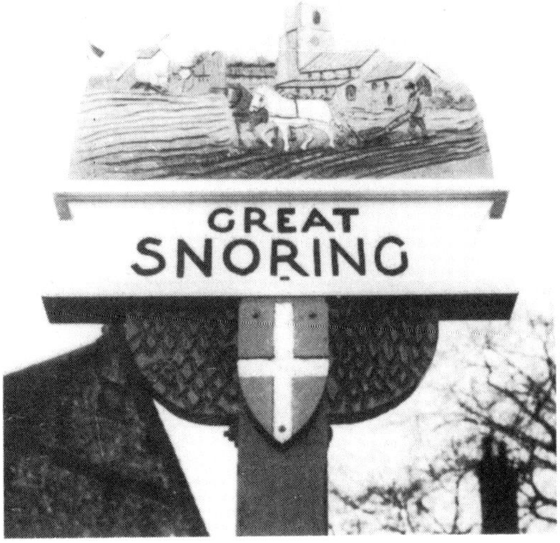
GREAT
SNORING

SOUTHERY

Southery, it appears, was once an island outpost, (the southern island) as was Hilgay, both low hills of clay in a vast area of swamp and fen.

It is now a considerable village on a gentle eminence surrounded still by fens, now drained and cultivated. In former times Southery even possessed a lighthouse as we see shown on the Village Sign.

Below the village is a bend in the river Ouse where a ferry used to ply and where wherries could call on their way to and from King's Lynn. There is still a Ferry Boat Inn which is obviously a popular meeting place. A windmill also stood upon the hill not far from the church and would have presented a welcome landmark to any travellers as it sails merrily turned. It must have caught all the winds of heaven in such an exposed place as Southery.

All this has been captured by Mr. Harry Carter in his carving, and the Sign was presented by the local Women's Institute.

FENS AT SOUTHERY

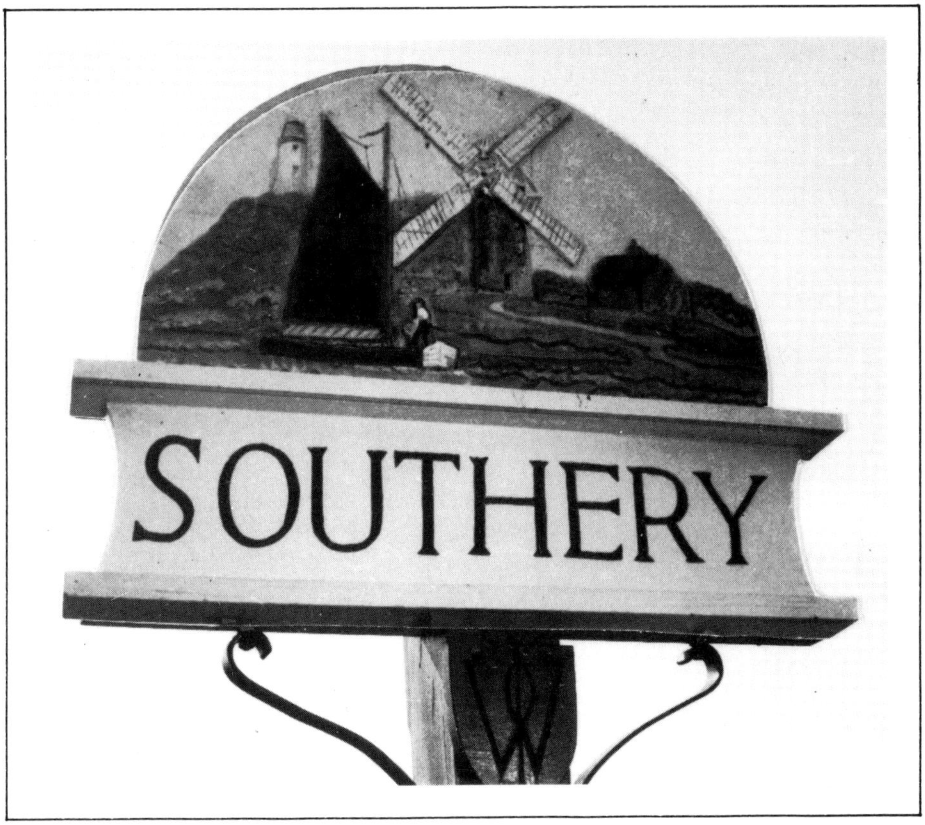
SOUTHERY

SPIXWORTH

Spixworth has developed mainly in the 20th century, from the few farms and houses bordering the road east of the Hall, to become a thriving community, spreading eastward to the parish boundary.

Spixworth's new Village Sign replaces the old one, of a crown upon a post, which commemorated the coronation of King George VI.

The Longe family, who lived in Spixworth Hall (now demolished), was connected with the village for over three hundred years and this has now been recognised and recorded in the new Sign by Mr. Harry Carter.

It was unveiled by Mr. Desmond Longe, High Sheriff of Norfolk and President of the Norwich Union, in August 1975. On the Sign is the coat of arms of the Longe family, with the motto "Pro fide et patria", — the family which has produced four High Sheriffs of Norfolk and many rectors of Spixworth, and which had fourteen members present at the opening ceremony!

Below the name is a picture of Spixworth Church with its unusual tower, which stands in a delightful rural setting. On the other shield is written "200 C", which indicates the village's 200 Club which raised most of the money for the Sign.

The Sign is well proportioned and has an attractive base of brick and flint.

SPIXWORTH

PRO FIDE AC PATRIA

SPIXWORTH

SPORLE

In a field near the church in Sporle, which is a small village built mainly along the one road not far from Swaffham, there can still be seen a few remants of masonry — all that is left of a Benedictine Priory that was built here in former times. It has also been suggested that the few visible stones mark the entrance to a tunnel from the Priory to the Church of St. Mary, part of which has traces of Norman work.

The Priory is supposed to have been founded in the time of Henry II (formerly Earl of Anjou) as a cell to the Abbey of St. Florence at Saumers in the province of Anjou. The churches of Sporle and of Palgrave were appropriated to it, and in 1219 it was valued at 8/6, having possessions by then in four parishes. The Priory was dissolved in 1461. Later it was given by Henry VI to Eton College.

The living of the church is still in the hands of Eton College.

The reconstruction of the Priory stands boldly on the Village Sign which was presented by the Women's Institute in 1972 and which is the work of Mr. Harry Carter of Swaffham. The village name has been carried out in particularly beautiful Roman capitals.

Priory Farm still stands beside the road opposite the Sign.

HARE HOUSE - SPORLE

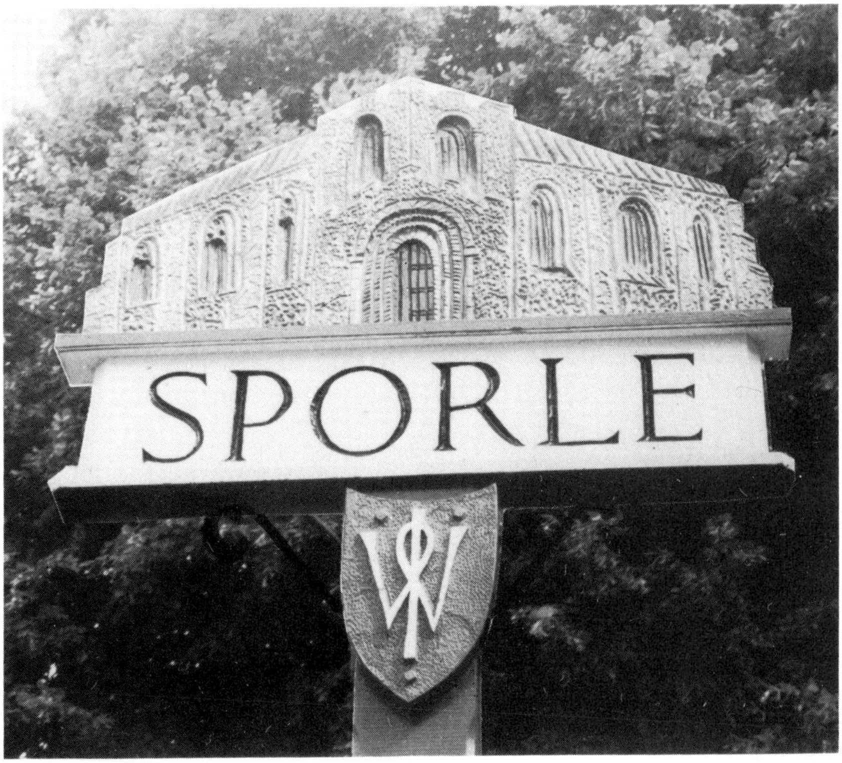
SPORLE

STANHOE

The attractive part of Stanhoe village, which lies about two miles east of Docking, is where the mellowed flint and pantile cottages are reflected in the village pond. In early summer ducks and moorhens and their fluffy little broods are intriguing and very accessible, often sunbathing in the grass almost on the road itself.

Beside the pond, where the verge is wider, stands the Village Sign, which was carved by a local craftsman, Mr. John Row. It shows the head of Sir Harvey de Stanhoe (1240-1300) who was a High Court Judge and Sheriff of Norfolk. Opposite is the outline of the church of All Saints showing its notable three-light window. In between these is emblazoned the Stanhoe coat of arms.

Below, in the spandrels, we see on the right a ploughman at work on a stony hill, (Stan-hoe) while in the left spandrel is a water carrier, with pails suspended from his yoke, a reminder of earlier ways before piped water was brought to the village. On the post are carved the village name and various flint implements, like those found in the vicinity of an ancient flint factory here in Stanhoe. There was once a flint mine on Massingham Heath in the neighbouring parish.

The cost of the Sign was raised by contributions from the local people, and a generous gift from Mr. Leverton, a new resident, who suggested the sign. The flint base was also local work, and built by Mr. Shackcloth.

STANHOE

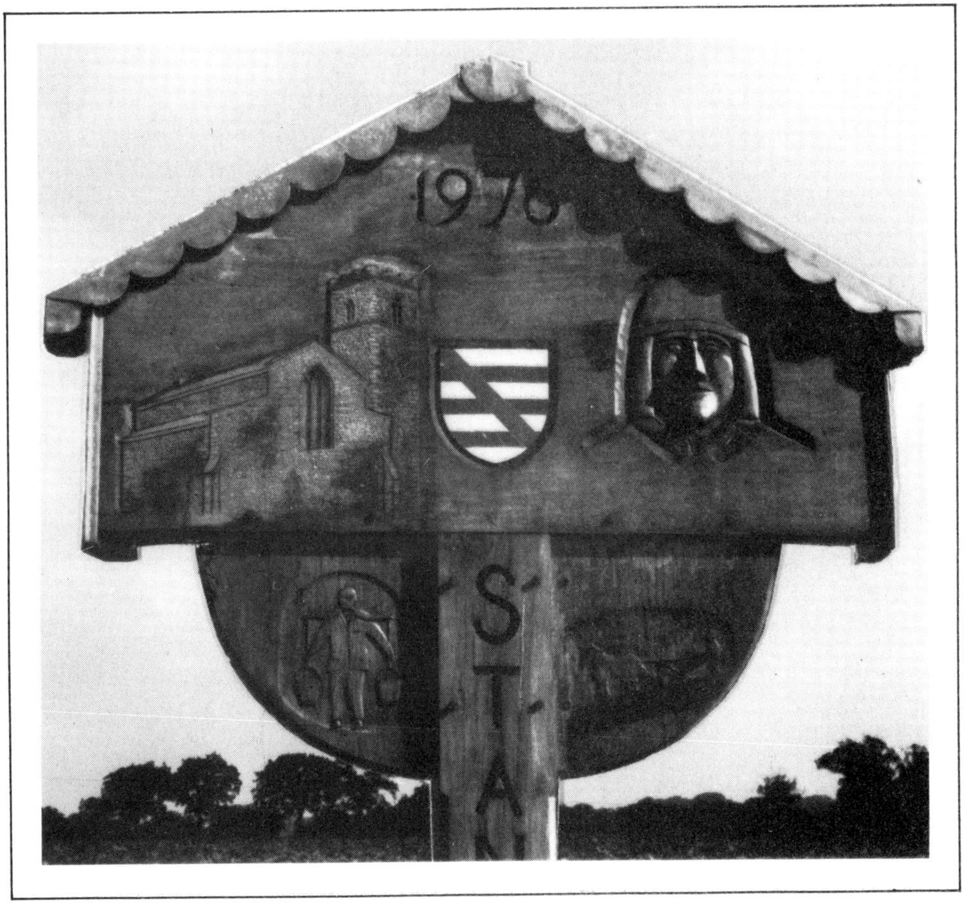
1976
S
T
A

STIBBARD

This quiet, dignified, and rather scattered village, in the heart of agricultural country has a most arresting and original sign, and in all the county there is not another even remotely like it. At first glance you might feel repelled, even taken aback by it — so different is it from the usual carved and painted wooden kind. But you cannot stop looking at it again and again, and giving it much serious thought; and you might, eventually like it more than any of the others.

Here is a gaunt, strange figure of a man, contrived from old pieces of farm machinery and implements — such as horse shoes, branding irons, hoes, forks and hinges to name but a few; and on his head he wears a battered old hat contrived from a first world-war helmet. It all sounds hard and grotesque, but how skilfully the artist had welded it together to make you see from his purposeful figure of the patient, hardworking ploughman guiding his single-furrow plough (itself a genuine relic) on and on, painstakingly and unremittingly, despite weariness, to till the earth so that it may bring forth our daily bread — as he has done from time immemorial. One's heart goes out to him, and he seems to become very real and human!

Those of you who are familiar with Edmund Blunden's very fine poetry may call to mind his poem "The Forefathers" — and henceforth link the two together, and see his life through the centuries — the warm, lovable countryman, with his work and pleasures, and deeply rooted attachment to the soil and his village life.

Stibbard is to be congratulated on having such an original sign, which by breaking away from the traditional type achieves its function so admirably and sympathetically.

STIBBARD

It was designed, and carried out by a newcomer to the village, who is a sculptress of international renown — Ros Newman — who has thus blended together old and new in a modern approach — and brought dignity and recognition to the humble ploughman, who is the very backbone of our great agricultural heritage.

The sign stands on a handsome brick platform, and is set in a landscaped piece of ground with a delightful setting of rosebeds about it.

It was erected by the Stibbard and District Women's Institute to celebrate the Queen's Silver Jubilee, and their own Golden Jubilee.

STIFFKEY

It is a matter for continual wonder how so many places with much in common can produce such a variety of themes for their village signs. There is a saying in Norfolk "du different", and one that the University of East Anglia has adopted for its motto on their coat of arms. And certainly as regards topics for their village signs the people of Norfolk do their best to live up to it so successfully that these new signs, as they are unveiled, perpetually intrigue one by their very originality.

Stiffkey is just such a place. It lies on the main coast road which goes from Wells to Blakeney. It is unspoilt and unsophisticated, with the road and the river winding through the wide sweeps and curves and sloping woods of the narrow valley of Stiffkey. And always in the distance — though unseen — is the sea!

Stiffkey is well known for its famous cockles called "Stewkey blues"; and here let it be said that the name of the place and river and valley, is pronounced by the residents as it is written — Stiffkey, not "stewkey" — a common confusion.

The cockle shells which range from pale to dark blue, are so coloured on account of a chemical reaction with the muddy sand out of which they are dug.

The intriguing and original village sign shows in the picture, women, in traditional dress, gathering cockles in the muddy flats. Behind and around them there is a shape like that of a large shell, a device of the artist, enclosing them in a kind of frame. On the sign there are various emblems — a marsh flower, and samphire, a succulent green plant, which grows on the marshes or sometimes on rock, and is both nourishing and delicious to eat. The emblems of St. John and St. Mary refer to two churches which were built so close to each other that ultimately they were joined together. The silver chalice is in the possession of the church. Lastly, the pig or boar is an emblem which refers to the Bacon family. Sir Nicholas Bacon lived in the manor, and bought the land which he gave to his son Nathaniel on which to build the hall. (Sir Francis Bacon was a much younger half-brother).

STIFFKEY

The sign was a gift from the local Women's Institute; who commissioned Mr. Harry Carter to make it. It was designed by Miss Joy Schwabe; and the base was constructed by Mr. John Pearson of flint cobbles and brick. The boy's head in the base was unearthed in a garden in Cambridge by Mr. Philip Schwabe and though it looks interesting has no particular bearing on the sign or local history.

STOKE FERRY

Stoke Ferry is a small and very busy town on the river Wissey, and it did once have a ferry. In the time of Henry III the Abbots of Ely, who received the profits of the ferry service, broke down the bridge which had not long been erected! But the Hundred Court compelled them to rebuild it. Below the name on the Village Sign can be seen a reminder of those days, with the ferryman in his boat poling across the blue water.

The main theme of the Sign, however, is about a considerable benefactor to the town, one James Bradfield, who by his will had erected and endowed in 1819 a free school for twenty-five poor boys, giving £250 for the building and £25 a year for the school-master. Another Bradfield later became Lord of the Manor in Stoke Ferry.

There is a Bradfield Trust of £1200, realising annually £30 (see 1922 Directory) which is administered for the benefit of Bradfield's Church of England School.

As you will see from the monogram on the Sign, it was provided by the local Women's Institute in celebration of its 50th anniversary in 1976, and was made by Mr. Harry Carter of Swaffham. Mr. Ernest Manning, a local craftsman built the base.

AT STOKE FERRY 1978

STOKE FERRY

SUTTON

Sutton is situated on the Northern fringe of Broadland, and, incidentally, only a few miles from the coast. It has a very pleasing sign, placed on a charming little reserve of green by the roadside.

Sutton was at one time on a broad, but during the last 100 years it has been gradually overgrown, so it would be useless to look for a broad now, nevertheless a dyke leads to the village from the river Ant, so Sutton is not far removed from all the delights of river and broads activities. When you see the sign itself, you will not be surprised to find on it, a wherry on a river, meaning, in this case that not only did they sail up to here, but that they were actually built here also. But now, alas, wherries are things of the past, save for one wherry still under sail, which is, as it were, a museum piece, owned and restored by the Norfolk Wherry Trust, and it still commands admiration and gives delight to those who see its great black sail as it moves majestically over the water. The sign also shows the magnificent windmill of Sutton, which is now the highest existing windmill in the country. It has recently been restored and is available to the public to inspect, and will, if it does not already, grind corn again as it did in its heyday.

The sign was erected in the Silver Jubilee year, and was presented by the Sutton Women's Institute, which at the same time had three trees planted nearby. The sign was carved and painted by Mr. Harry Carter, and it will no doubt be the object of much interest and give great pleasure. It is mounted on a strong post, and has a circular seat around it. The firm Banesters of Stalham was responsible for the building and erection of the sign.

SUTTON

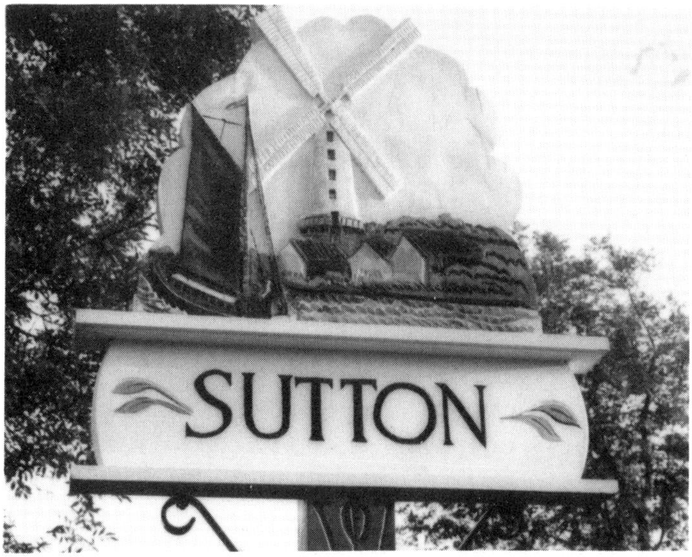
SUTTON

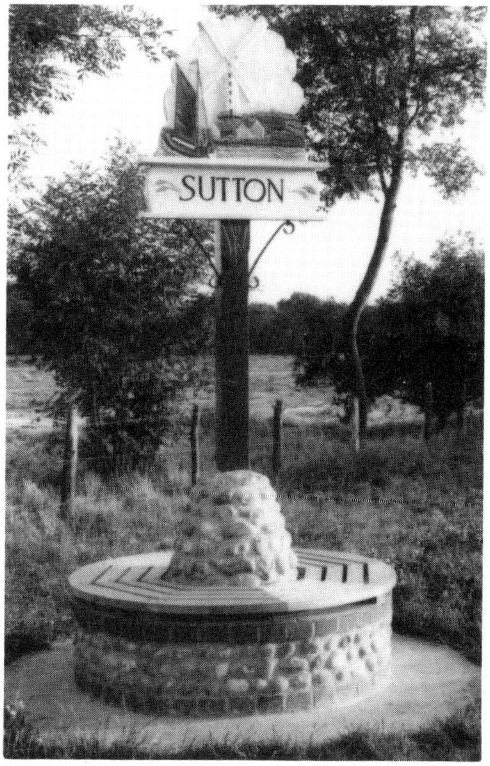
SUTTON

SWAINSTHORPE

This is another of those villages which is mentioned in Domesday Book, but which otherwise, according to its village sign, lays no claim to being of historical interest. It is a rather scattered village, through one part of which the main highway passes, and has on it some gabled houses, and a C17 Inn, named "The Dun Cow". A smaller road branching off it leads to the church, and more houses, both old and new, and a main line railway line cuts through it, but no longer serves the locality as formerly. It is a typical, homely Norfolk village and must surely be a pleasant place to live in.

The village sign is to be found on a small green outside the parish church, which is a striking building with its Norman tower, and having an interesting interior also. The sign is semi-circular in shape, on which is a fine painting of a man guiding a plough drawn by two horses with the church behind them. It is well placed and suitably mounted and is sure to appeal to viewers, with its attractive and glowing appearance.

The name Swainsthorpe is of old Danish derivation, and means "Svein's settlement or farm" — so once again we are in a village which once fell into the hands of the Vikings — for at that time all East Anglia was easily accessible from the sea, having only weak and scattered defences at the best, and the Vikings were an immensely strong and utterly ruthless foe, against which the local people were no match, and were insufficiently armed. But East Anglia was not the only objective, for many other parts of the coastline of Britain, and even Europe itself, were constantly under attack. The sign was made by Mr. Harry Carter, and was paid for by parishioners and house to house collections by Mrs. S. Cree and Mr. A. Stevenson. The base was constructed by Mr. M. Shea, and the sign was erected to mark the occasion of the Queen's Silver Jubilee.

SWAINSTHORPE

SWAINSTHORPE

TERRINGTON St. Clement and Terrington St. John

The name Terrington derives from the Saxon, and is mentioned in Domesday Book; it means the Tun of Tir's people. At one time both these places were one parish, until 1843, when the benefice of St. John's was separated from St. Clement, and is now a perpetual curacy. The two places are a little over three miles apart, but obviously share the same history. They lie in the marshland 6 miles west of King's Lynn. This area of land around the Wash is very low-lying, indeed it seems that the sea is a perpetual menace, and it needs cautious and ceaseless guarding against inundation and flooding. As far back as Roman times defences were built to keep the sea out; and since then, centuries later, English men and Dutch men have played their part in using all their ingenuity and skill to build embankments and to dig dykes to drain away the water. But at no time has man ever been able to say that he has control of the situation; and vigilance will always be needed; for when tides and winds threaten to combine to flood over this vast low-lying area, then man must needs to be well equipped and most resourceful to control flooding and devastation.

TERRINGTON ST. CLEMENT

Terrington St. Clement lies on the main road from Sleaford to King's Lynn (the A17), and is a large well populated village with a truly magnificent church which has been very aptly named "The Cathedral of the Marshes", and its interior is as beautiful as its exterior.

This area is famous for its fruit farming as well as other crops, owing to its rich and fertile soil.

There is a very striking and handsome village sign, which stands in a good position, where a minor road branches off from the main road towards the church. It is double-sided with both sides alike. It takes the form of a large shield, taken from a hatchment in the village church, and indicates the coat of arms of the Hamond family, one member of whom owned property here in Terrington and was an outstanding naval officer, and a baronet, namely Sir Andrew Snape Hamond. His only son also entered the navy and became Admiral of the Fleet

TERRINGTON ST CLEMENT

in 1862. Below the shield there is a motto in Latin, which translated means "Ready and Faithful". In the spandrels may be seen strawberries and sheep which means that fruit farming and sheep rearing have been, in their time, the main sources of wealth in the locality. Although fruit is grown plentifully now, the sheep refer to past times when Norfolk was famous for its weaving of fine woollen cloth, and when vast areas were given over to the rearing of sheep from whose fleeces the wool was obtained.

The sign was the gift of the Terrington St. Clement's Women's Institute, who commissioned Mr. Harry Carter to make it.

TERRINGTON ST. JOHN

To know something of the history of a place, and to study an old map of it, helps one to know — with understanding — so much that would otherwise remain obscure. The Terringtons have a distinct character of their own, and one can appreciate why Terrington St. John is an independent village; for lying three miles apart, its church (built in the C14), must first of all been a chapel of ease for Terrington St. Clement, and because in those days people went more frequently to attend their own church it must have saved them many weary miles of constant coming and going. The nature of the place was quiet and remote, for whereas there are now countless fields where many crops of all kinds are grown, formerly this was a large area of commonland, crossed and recrossed by small lanes, thus enabling the villagers to reach every part on which the people grazed their animals. So looking at the informative village sign we can see that in the parish of St. John — the patron saint of their church, the horse and sheep and geese (and doubtless goats and donkeys and other livestock) were all grazed by right and kept in their appointed places.

How quiet and unhurried it was in those times — and what a contrast compared with our present restless pace! The main road which was made to go from King's Lynn to Wisbech, cuts directly through this old common land, and modern farming has covered the old grazing lands; a stream of traffic roars ceaselessly along the main road, nonstop day and night, so much so that the cheerful and friendly little village sign seems to have taken fright, and to avoid being a casualty has taken refuge on the edge of a field, with a ditch and a low hedge between it and the hostile traffic! It is not so easy to see its two (similar) sides there, but it was probably a wise choice for a site in the circumstances!

The sign was designed by Mr. Colin Dawson, and Mr. Walker of King's Lynn, using Japanese oak (which is fine grained but pleasant to manipulate), very ably carved and painted it. It was contributed to as a village "rejoicing" for the Queen's Silver Jubilee, which was apparently an occasion not likely to be forgotten for many a long year.

TERRINGTON ST JOHN

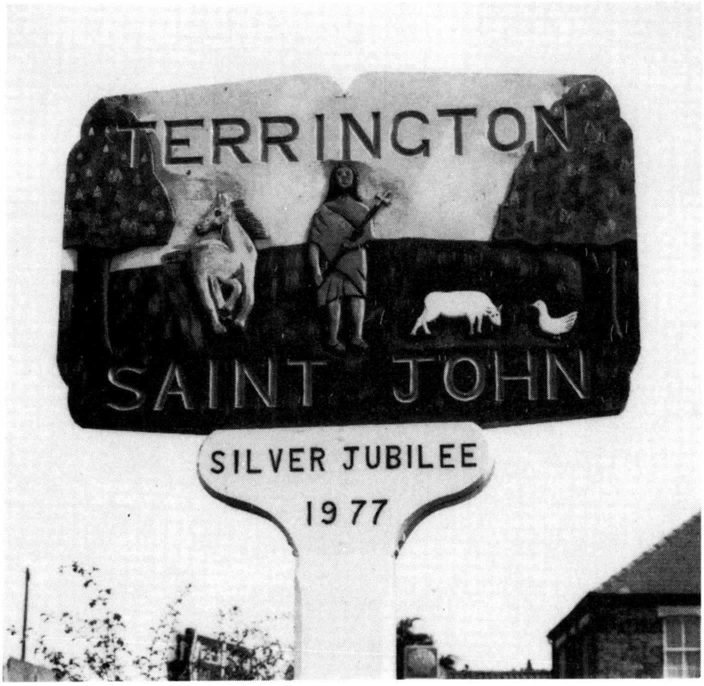
TERRINGTON
SAINT JOHN
SILVER JUBILEE
1977

THORPE END GARDEN VILLAGE

In our first book "Village and Town Signs in Norfolk", you will see a photograph of the sign as it was then — a beautifully rendered little oak tree, set within a close triangular framework carved in wood and standing beside a wooden seat. This original design has been incorporated within a larger one, which shows a man and a woman gardening, he digging, and she watering the plants. This is also contained within a very decorative wrought iron frame. There is no background, so the design stands out clearly in silhouette, which has a very attractive effect. This adaptation brings the sign up to date and applies to the Thorpe End appelation the "Garden Village", and shows its development. and also celebrates the Queen's Silver Jubilee in this clear and comprehensive way, as well as the Diamond Jubilee, in the following year, of the Women's Institute, whose members gave the sign to the village.

The original design was made by Mr. John Chaplin, the architect who had earlier designed many of the houses at Thorpe End.

For the updated sign, plans were submitted by Mr. Kenneth Jay, who did the work and also made the plaques from the design made by Mr. David Whiting. Mr. John Harmer, a builder in Thorpe End made the very suitable cobble and brick plinth on which it stands.

This delightful sign, therefore, is a product of local talent. It is a striking sign to photograph, particularly in the evening when the sun is setting, thus giving a dramatic effect to it, and enhancing the restrained and pleasing colours of the figures.

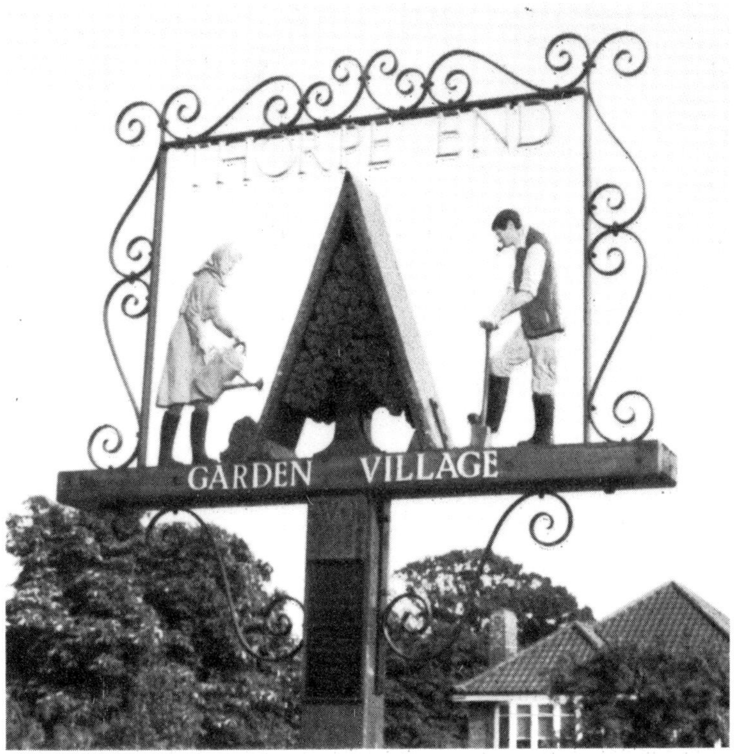
GARDEN VILLAGE

THORPE MARKET

On the A149 road from North Walsham to Cromer, one passes through Thorpe Market. It is a small and delightful village, quiet and dignified, with many of its thatched houses and cottages fringing the green. There is one house in particular which is obviously of outstanding architectural merit; it is Elizabethan in period, and built in flint, with stepped gables flanking a stepped porch, and with impressive decorative chimneys; it is known as Green Farm House, and stands opposite the green, on which is erected the very pleasing and well designed village sign. It is made of oak, in the shape of a large cross, and is surmounted by an iron circle containing a double sided round panel, and over it is a large curved name plate, out of which is cut the words Thorpe Market, and this again is surrounded by very graceful iron scroll work. The circular panels represent two close associations with the village, one with the Lord of the Manor, namely Lord Suffield, and his family, who lived at Gunton Hall, nearby. The Suffields had a close friendship with King Edward VII, who enjoyed his visits to their home which, with its fine parklands was so suited to the pursuits of leisured people, being well-stocked with game and fish. But the significance to us of King Edward is that he was the originator of village signs, and inaugurated them by having the very first ones of all erected around his own estate at Sandringham. We have reason to be grateful for his inspiration for it has given many people great pleasure and a lively interest within our own county boundary, and has influenced other counties as well to emulate us — as well as stimulated a deeper interest in local history, customs, and folklore, etc. On the reverse side of the panel is a picture of a ploughing scene in Saxon times, whilst the picture of two pheasants in the park brings the history of the village up to more recent times.

The sign was erected by the people of the village to commemorate the occasion of the Queen's Silver Jubilee; and all those who contributed to it should be congratulated on achieving a most creditable result; in particular these include,

THORPE MARKET

from the plinth upwards:- Mr. A. Gentry and Mr. G. Bowles for supplying the materials and building the base; Mr. C. Davies for the fine iron-work which so well sets off the whole sign; Mr. D. Cooper for the first-class painting on either side of the panel; and to The Hon. Miss Doris Harbord, a descendant of the Suffield family, for so kindly presenting the oak on which to erect the sign, and of which we are reminded by the acorn and leaves at the top.

THREE HOLES

Not far from Outwell and Upwell on the western border of Norfolk is a hamlet with the strange name of Three Holes, once called Three Holes Bridge. It lies near a fenland drain called Popham's Eau, which led eventually to Well Creek and the Ouse, and was navigable to King's Lynn.

Where this stream used to pass under the main road was a bridge with three holes, or arches, with three sluices below them. Recently however a short section has been abandoned and a new channel constructed to join the Middle Level drain just before the modern iron bridge a little further south. The original stream, no more than a trickle, has almost disappeared, and rough undergrowth and bushes fill the old channel. The new drains are ruler-straight for miles, wide and clear of vegetation.

However this little community has its own Village Sign. It takes the form of a bridge carved in oak with three circular openings, and half hidden by the bridge coping is a fisherman, complete with rod and line, and also a horse, its driver and his loaded wagon.

The sign was carved and painted by Mr. Harry Carter and funds were raised by the villagers, including the Women's Institute, over twelve months in the Jubilee Year, to commemorate the Silver Jubilee of the Queen and of the local Women's Institute at the same time.

THREE HOLES

THREE HOLES

1952
1977

THURTON

Thurton is one of those villages which, unfortunately, is bisected by a busy main road, having its church, one inn, the foundry and some dwellings on one side, and shop, school and more houses on the other, including some by the architects Taylor and Greene as well as being sited at a crossroads in the dip between two hills. It is however a pretty village in the heart of farming country, and the local Women's Institute, combined with that of Ashby and district, raised funds over some three years toward a Village Sign to commemorate their Jubilee.

A site on the boundary of the two villages on the crest of the hill was approved, and the unveiling ceremony on a sunny evening in July 1976 was a most successful climax.

Mr. Harry Carter, now renowned for his sign-making, was approached and shown the church of St. Ethelbert in Thurton with its fine stained glass windows, said to have come from Rouen, when they were sold during the time of the French Revolution. He was most impressed, and based his ideas on them, with St. Ethelbert in the centre. The other two figures in white robes with heraldic shields above them balance the design.

Much appreciation was expressed not only to the former president, Mrs. Leathers, but to all others concerned, including the local firms of Youngs (of Chedgrave) and Capps (of Thurton) who made the plinth and plaque.

THURTON

THURTON

THWAITE ST. MARY

The small, secluded. and very pretty hamlet of Thwaite St. Mary lies about 12 miles south of Norwich. It is set in the midst of purely agricultural country, and has never varied greatly either in its size or in the number of its inhabitants. It has a most attractive and impressive village sign, which stands on a bank at the T junction of two roads in the centre of the hamlet. It takes the form of a small size replica of the Norman doorway of its parish church. and is beautifully carved in natural coloured oak; so one is quite obviously drawn to see the original, which is close by, and well worth a visit. Here one gets a great surprise, for below its delightfully thatched roof, and tall tower, the doorway itself is Norman and all the rest of the church is of a much later date, and is as plain and undecorated as the doorway is ornate. Of the early history of the church, or who was responsible for building it, there is no record at all; but this much is clear, and that is that its stone must have been brought here at the same time that Norwich cathedral was being built, and most likely from the same source, namely Caen, and that it was likewise conveyed by water to the nearest wharf and landing place, as could be found.

The word thwaite is of Scandinavian origin, and means an enclosure or clearing. So the place has lived through at least two invasions — those of the Vikings and the Normans. But despite these eventful happenings over the centuries one thing has remained unchanged — and probably uninterrupted, namely the age-old occupation of agriculture.

The sign was made by Mr. C. Reeve of Mettingham, who has several others to his credit, most notably the very beautiful sign at Geldeston, which is still one of the finest in the county.

THWAITE

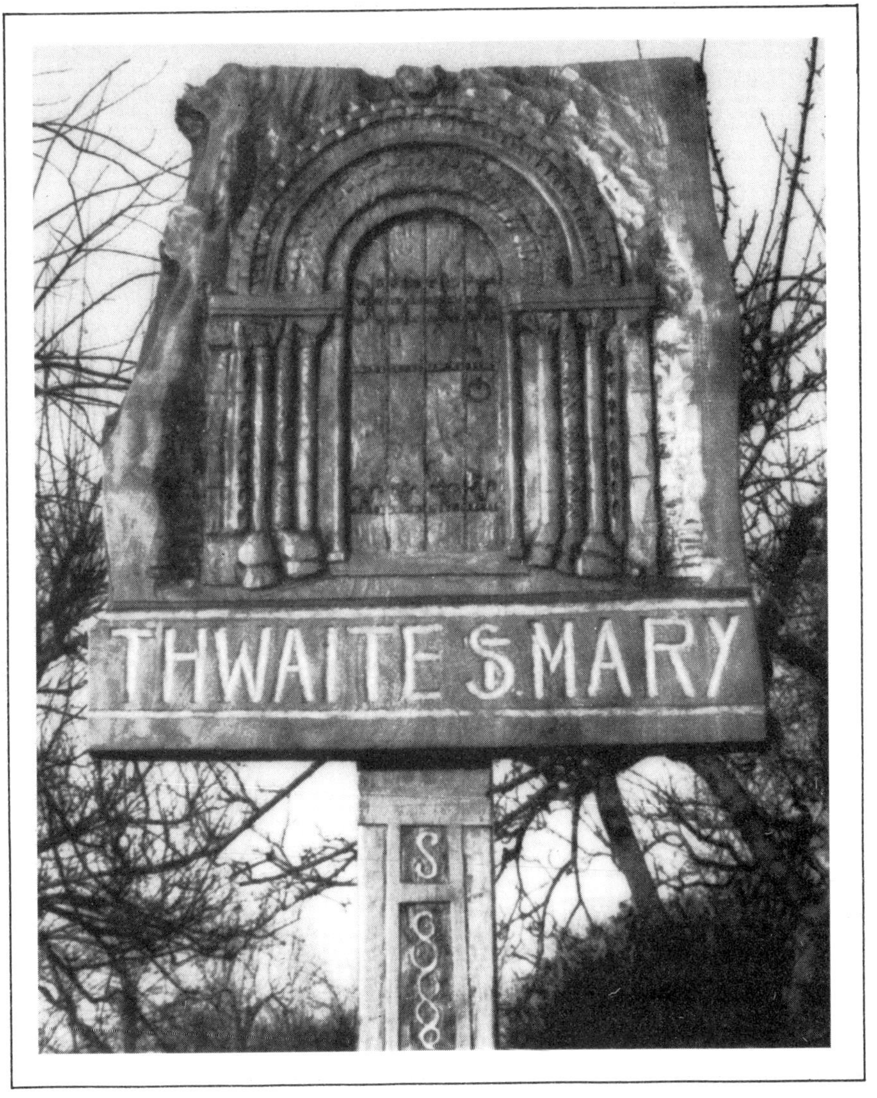
THWAITE ST MARY

TILNEY ALL SAINTS

In the marshlands of West Norfolk (not to be confused with the fens which lie some miles southward) is to be found the lovely old Norman church of Tilney All Saints set in the midst of a pretty, small village, all in a quiet backwater off the noisy, busy, lorry-laden main road. It is here that in a grave of about nine feet in length, outside the chancel, lies the body of Frederic de Tilney, a man renowned for his great size and strength. He went on the Crusades with Richard Coeur de Lion, who knighted him for his brave deeds. Later he was killed at Acre, and his body was brought home for burial to Tilney All Saints. There is a local legend of a giant named Hicafric or Hickathrift, who used a wheel for a shield, and an axle for a weapon. He is reputed, in anger, to have hurled a massive stone for about three miles, hitting a church and damaging the wall. Sir Frederic is said to have had a large flock of sheep on his lands, and he could easily in defence of his property, or himself, have snatched the nearest things to hand and have used a wheel to defend himself and an axle as a weapon against the offenders. And as for the story of the stone throwing incident, it is highly unlikely to say the least of it, and proves nothing you must admit! But the name Hickafric could easily be a corruption of Frederic — thus suggesting that Hickafric and Frederic were one and the same person, and that the truth gave rise to the fable. It is anybody's guess of course, and you may think otherwise. Nevertheless in the church there is also a stone coffin lid, some eight feet long, with cross patterning upon it and that does prove that a giant of a man had reality after all!

The village sign was designed by Mrs. Middleton, made by Mr. Harry Carter and was a gift of the local Women's Institute erected to commemorate the Queen's Silver Jubilee. It is a bright and cheerful looking sign, and claims one's attention

TILNEY ALL SAINTS

instantaneously. It shows, against the background of the village church, a great man, with a wheel close to him, holding in both hands an axle-tree. On the right side are to be seen some growing corn, and root crops, to remind one that here, too, agriculture is the main occupation. A small panel beneath the sign bears the emblem of the W.I. It stands outside the churchyard wall, on a handsome plinth of sandstone blocks.

It is interesting to have another example to add to our stories of witches, spectral dogs, hauntings, and things that go bump in the night!

TILNEY ST. LAWRENCE

Tilney St. Lawrence is one of the marshland villages in the west of Norfolk. It stretches along each arm of the crossroads south of its church and Hall, and just off the main road between King's Lynn and Wisbech.

On the corner is the Village Sign. Two figures stand below the name board, one representing the patron saint of the church. and the other John Aylmer, who was born at Aylmer Hall, and became friend and tutor to Lady Jane Grey, whose scholarship was considerable. He fled the country during the reign of Mary Tudor, but returned in that of Elizabeth I. In 1577 John Aylmer became Bishop of London, but his character had changed and he was increasingly disliked. He died in 1594 and was buried in old St. Paul's.

St. Lawrence, opposite John Aylmer, was regarded from the 4th century as one of the greatest saints of Rome, who was cruelly put to death, some say roasted on a gridiron, all because when asked to produce the valuables of the church he brought forward the poor and sick and said "Here are the church's treasures". Thus our two figures represent the academic and the spiritual, whereas the other features are concerned with the local environment.

Above the name board is a symbol of the wheel of industry, past and present. The spokes are made up of a crook, denoting sheep farming in the past, a whip, symbolic of cattle drovers and horse-drawn traffic of more recent times, and the spanner, as well as the wheel itself, which is composed in part of a cogwheel and in part of a tyre, suggests modern farm machinery made nearby, as well as road haulage of today.

AYLMER HALL (TODAY)
TILNEY ST LAWRENCE

At the base of the post are bullrushes, reminding us of the days when the area was a watery waste, instead of fields and the fertile acres we see today.

The design for the Sign was the result of a local competition which was won by Mrs. Carter. It was carried out by Mr. Walker, a skilled craftsman, who once carved fair-ground horses for the roundabouts, at the well-known firm of Messrs. Savage of King's Lynn. The Sign was erected in 1974.

TITTLESHALL

Tittleshall is an attractive village with a fine church built mainly of flint, as are many of the dwellings, a common feature in many of our Norfolk villages.

The Village Sign was one of the simpler ones put up to mark the Coronation of Queen Elizabeth II, but what it lacks in decoration is compensated by its successful functional design. The name is clear and makes immediate impact, while the upkeep must be minimal.

The original site chosen at the entrance to the village was a happy one, for the view ahead was inviting to the visitor. However, sometime during 1977 the Sign was moved to a more central position and provided with a base of flint cobbles, and a plaque was added too, to record and commemorate the Queen's Silver Jubilee.

Tittleshall can lay claim to fame in that several of the Coke family lie buried in the church — Sir Edward Coke, both famous and infamous, who married Bridget Paston as his first wife. He was Lord Chief Justice of the King's Bench and died in 1634 — Thomas Coke who built Holkham Hall — and also the renowned "Coke of Norfolk", Earl of Leicester, agriculturalist, and Father of the House of Commons.

TITTLESHALL

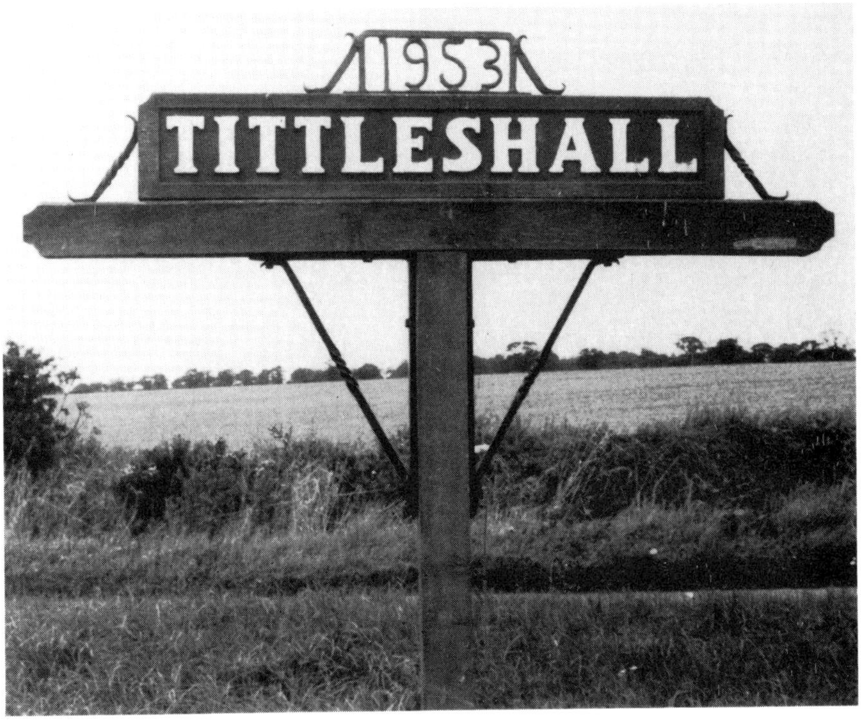
1953
TITTLESHALL

TRUNCH

There is no doubt that Trunch is a most attractive and interesting village. If you are a photographer you will find so many angles from which to take a picture, that you could spend a long time just taking advantage of all the opportunities that present themselves to your camera. In addition there is a very fine church, with a font cover of such incredible beauty that there are only three others to compare with it in all England; then there is a very lovely rood screen, and many other features such as a piscina and miserere seats to appeal to people interested in architecture. But, of course, it is very likely that you came here primarily to see the village sign, and here you will find a sign worthy of the village, of which it is the epitome; and contains much reference to the past of Trunch.

It is made of painted ironwork, and is a perfect example of its kind. It was designed by Mr. Eric Stevenson, himself the maker of many fine signs, and was carried out by Mr. Rodney Cranwell. It is most pleasing to the eye, and brings out clearly the most salient features of the village. There are three large symbols and two very much smaller ones. In the centre the church of St. Botolph is shown, with its great tall tower; on the left the brewery is represented, a building which was erected in 1837, and was a flourishing concern in those days; whilst on the right a tractor and plough are to be seen, the symbols we are used to seeing which always represents agriculture, and which has been going on here throughout past centuries. On either side of the name are the two much smaller emblems, on the left is the village pump, and on the right a mere "hint" of the very beautiful font cover already mentioned.

TRUNCH

Lastly the sign stands on a most adequate base very skilfully constructed by Mr. W. Self. The sign was erected in 1977, the year of the Queen's Silver Jubilee. It was paid for by generous donations from Mr. Harry Geary and other members of the parish.

UPTON with Fishley

Upton village lies around a cluster of roads in the quiet countryside some three miles from Acle, with access to the Bure via Upton Dyke. Its houses span several centuries and include a good many pleasant modern homes too, having developed considerably in recent years. Not far away is Fishley, with little more than the church and Hall and a few other dwellings in its parish.

Upton and Fishley were united in 1831, and they now possess an attractive Village Sign, very well placed in a sheltered hedgerow. On each side has been built, by Mr. Warner, a local resident, inviting seats of applewood, making a pleasant rendezvous for village folk and visiting yachtsmen.

For many years the Norwich Union Life Insurance Society has owned land in the area and taken an interest in the village, in fact the company provided the cost of the Sign which was made by Mr. Harry Carter of Swaffham and unveiled in July 1976.

The Sign shows St. Margaret's Church at Upton which in 1550 was almost destroyed by a storm, the tower was only rebuilt in 1928-9. A windmill recalls the older type of corn mill. Both villages possessed a mill.

In the past wherries carried coal from the port of Yarmouth and returned with grain from the countryside using the village wharves as well as the larger quays.

Also on the Sign a farmer is busily ploughing the field in preparation for next year's crops.

UPTON DYKE

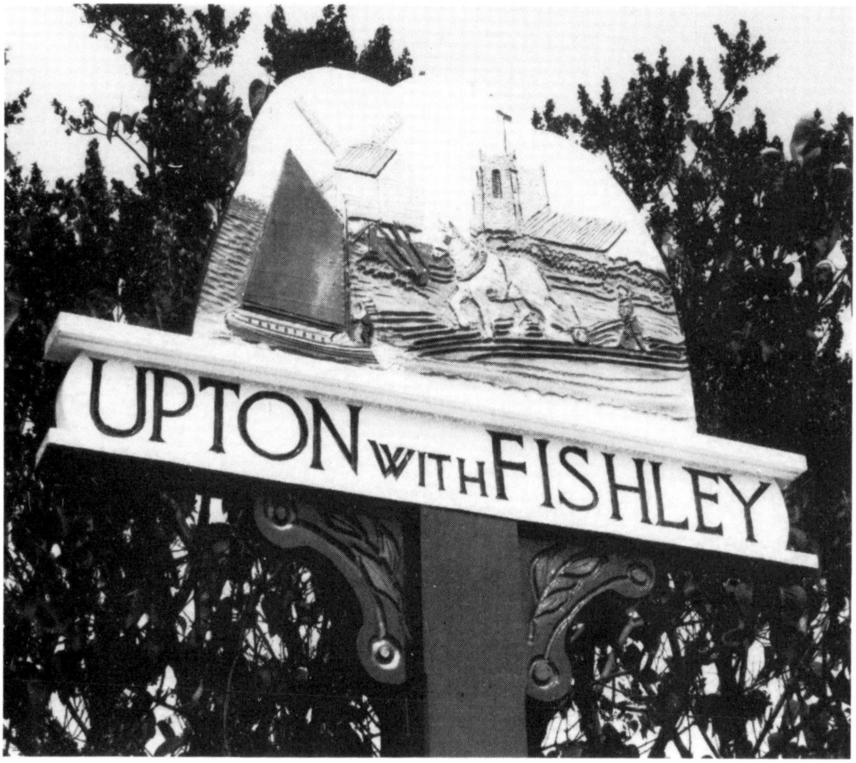
UPTON WITH FISHLEY

SOUTH WALSHAM

South Walsham is a pleasant little village amply endowed with fine trees, not far from one of the more attractive Broads connected with the river Bure, and only about a mile from its sister boating centre at Ranworth.

Far back in history, when there were many Danish incursions into Norfolk, at first near the coast, and later further inland, by way of the rivers; South Walsham people, like those of other Saxon settlements, no doubt lived in fear of those terrible Northern invaders. On South Walsham's Village Sign can be seen a Danish ship sailing upstream. Behind it is a typical drainage mill and the towers of the two churches familiar to holiday invaders of the 2oth century. It was only a year or so ago that the tower of St. Lawrence, which had been left ruined after a fire in 1827, finally collapsed. A Saxon warrior watches from the near bank.

There is a legend about a ghostly Danish ship which is said to appear at midnight every May 1st, and which is then consumed by fire, re-enacting the funeral pyre of Oscar, a famous priest-king, who had sacked the village and lorded it over the inhabitants. He died there from being given the wrong kind of mushrooms — on purpose!

The Sign was given by the local Women's Institute, made by Mr. Harry Carter and erected in June 1975.

SOUTH WALSHAM

SOUTH WALSHAM

GREAT WALSINGHAM

Great Walsingham is an attractive hamlet in two sections, divided by the little River Stiffkey. Great Walsingham remains little, and Little Walsingham, a mile away, has expanded greatly, due to the many pilgrimages to the still famous shrine there.

Having won the award for the Best Kept Village in 1972, the Parish Council of Great Walsingham wished to mark the fact by erecting a permanent Village Sign. They defrayed 90% of the cost, and the remainder came from the rates. Mr. Harry Carter's skill was sought once more.

The Lee-Warner family were Lords of the Manor of both Great and Little Walsingham, and once lived in the great house where the Priory ruins now stand, known as Walsingham Abbey. During the 1880s there were at least six of the family living in the district, and an earlier member, Sir William Lee-Warner, was an eminent scholar and an authority on Indian affairs. His impressive tomb and that of his wife were both in Little Walsingham Church.

The idea of the Squirrel and the nut or acorn was taken from the Lee-Warner crest, and reminds us too of the great oak, dating from 1692 and still flourishing on the green triangle in the centre of Great (or Old) Walsingham.

The Sign was designed by Mr. Harrington of Little Walsingham and unveiled by Mrs. Emily Gentleman who has resided in Great Walsingham for 73 years. The base was made by Mr. Eric Seaman, Chairman of the Parish Council.

GREAT WALSINGHAM

GREAT WALSINGHAM

WINNER OF THE
BEST KEPT VILLAGE
COMPETITION
1972
FOR VILLAGES OVER 400 POPULATION
Presented by the Eastern Daily Press

WATLINGTON

The village of Watlington lies in pleasant and rich agricultural country on the edge of the fens, midway between King's Lynn and Downham Market. Its village sign stands on the edge of the village green, facing the "Angel" public house.

The large coloured scene on it shows the distribution of charity loaves to poor people, a reminder of a charity of £5. 4. 0, left by a parishioner named John Davies in 1747. It was the largest of several charities which amounted in all to £9.7.0. The charity was administered in the form of twelve small loaves given to poor widows, on alternate Sundays, half of them living in Watlington, and half in the neighbouring village of Tottenhill. It is a strange coincidence that the money came from the rents of a piece of land known as "Holybreads"!

This is the first sign to date on which a charity is taken as a main theme for the village sign. It is interesting that some recognition is given to the great need for charities, in perpetuity, by richer parishioners to the poor and needy in the past, before the time when the state was responsible for all that is done nowadays which we seem to take for granted. The only source of assistance then was the very meagre Poor Relief which only provided sufficient means to keep body and soul together. Even workhouses had not been thought of as yet. How very welcome then those loaves of bread, or coals, or clothing and so on, must have been to those unfortunate people.

The "Good old days" were not so good to all, quite obviously, and given the chance to exchange them for present day conditions would not be everybody's choice by any means!

The sign was erected by the Parish Council to commemorate the occasion of the Queen's Silver Jubilee.

It was made by Mr. Harry Carter and was paid for by donations from villagers and parishioners, and from money collected from fund raising events.

WATLINGTON

WELNEY

In the far-off corner of South-west Norfolk is situated Welney, one of several villages astride the old Croft river which divides our county from that of Cambridgeshire.

Here is true fenland country, and on the southern side of the village and only about half a mile apart are the two wide parallel drainage channels, the old and the new Bedford rivers, constructed to drain this part of the Fens. The cost was almost entirely borne by the then Earl of Bedford between 1630 and 1653.

The uninhabited land which lies between them is known as Welney Wash. For many years, when our winters were hard enough, this Wash became flooded and frozen, and skating there was popular. Many sporting events took place and great races were won. Norwegian long skates were introduced here in England, and speed rather than figure skating was the aim.

Also during winter months great congregations of wildfowl came to rest on their migrations, providing a welcome source of food for the fenman. Now a conservation area, with hides for bird-watchers, is provided for visitors such as Bewick swans and tufted ducks, which can be seen in great numbers, as well as many other varieties of water birds.

There were windmills too in the past, great landmarks in this flat, bleak region.

All these are shown on the tall Village Sign at Welney which stands on the site of an old well near the church of St. Mary. It was put up, we believe, in 1976. It has a car-stone base and was carved and painted by Mr. Harry Carter.

Below the village name is a monogram, the initials of William Marshall of Lincoln's Inn Fields, London, who in 1661 bequeathed nine pieces of land in trust for the benefit of the church, the poor, and the maintenace of the highways. Later the funds accrued and allowed for the provision of a free school which was built in 1848, and another in 1874.

If you go to Wereham there is little doubt that your memories of it will be of a very pleasant visit and you will come away remembering a delightful and amusing story that the village sign tells.

The village centre has the essential features all together, the houses, cottages and school clustered about its village green seemingly of the same period except the church, which is some centuries older. Much is completely Victorian, so it gives the impression of solidity and comfort; and one can imagine it in bitter wintry weather impervious to winds and storms; for the Victorians were great believers in making things very durable, and it has an air of security and permanence. Picture it, if you will, in the early spring, when everything looks fresh and cheerful, its village pond sparkling and fringed with drooping willows, and maybe from its village school you may see children emerging in colourful groups, their happy young voices carried on the light air. One can sit on the green, and glance across the road to observe the gay, swinging sign of the village pub which figures in the story.

But close at hand is the new village sign (recently made by Mr. Harry Carter), depicting in carved and painted wood, the figure of a young female saint — the virgin martyr, St. Margaret, holding a tall slender cross, and behind her is the village church. She is the patron of this C13 church — as she is of so many Norfolk churches.

But it is in the small spandrels that the main interest lies. In the right spandrel is a picture of the conduit which carries the water from St. Margaret's well to the pond (called "the pit" by the villagers) The spring was used as the principal water supply before the mains water was brought to the village, and which was at first rejected by the residents who preferred the plentiful supply from their own excellent well! On the left spandrel is a picture of "Billy the Seal", who was a local celebrity in his time; and his memory is still kept alive, some villagers still have treasured photos of him, and speak of him in a friendly way. About 60 years ago a resident of the parish found him in the Wash, rescued him, and brought him back to Wereham, and put him in the pond, where he lived happily for the rest of his long life. He soon endeared himself to children and adults alike, and so he became quite popular. His fame spread to surrounding villages, and gained him the name of "Billy the Seal". In fact he was quite a character! He had such social qualities that every evening he slithered across to the "George and Dragon" where he joined the locals in the bar and was treated to his pint regularly. Then, all in due time, he slithered back contentedly to his own watery domain!

WESTON LONGVILLE

This sign is a gift from the 566th Bomber Group of the 8th American Air Force which was stationed at Attlebridge, adjoining Weston Longville. Other memorials were also given to the church.

During the last World War a total of 344 airmen lost their lives during the 20 months that the group was on flight operations — 314 of them died in the months that the group were flying from Attlebridge. Some local people, will, of course, remember them, but a new, younger generation will have grown up to whom this enormous sacrifice of young men of the same age as themselves may, we hope, be more fully realised by this generous gift to their own village.

The sign is shaped roughly in a V shape, with the name Weston Longville over the top. In it are three shields, the one on the top left is of New College, Oxford. This is because New College held the gift of the "living" there. The one on the right was of the Rookwood, or according to the old spelling, Rokewood family, to whom the estate belonged before the Custances came into possession of it. The village, small but very attractive, was where Parson James Woodforde lived for the last 43 years of his life after he became the incumbent, his appointment being made in 1793 by his own college of St. John's at Oxford, from 1760 to 1803, when he died. He was a kindly, lovable man who lived among his parishioners, knowing each one personally, and really caring for them individually. He kept a diary for 43 years, which until nearly sixty years ago was unknown. He wrote it only for his own edification, and mentioned all the incidents — large and small — which concerned himself and those about him with such candour and simplicity that it is most intriguing to read and gives a perfectly authentic commentary of country life in the C18 and C19. It is a diary which ranks with the greatest diaries in the English language.

WESTON LONGVILLE

Whilst living in Weston Longville he became very friendly with the Custances who owned, and lived at the Hall, a building set in beautiful parkland, and the shield of the Custance family is the third one on the sign. The hall was demolished some time ago, also the rectory — so that visitors will find no focal point in the village with which to connect them save the church where the Rokewoods, the Custances, Parson Woodforde and the American Air Force men are all duly remembered.

WICKLEWOOD

This sign stands on the main road from Dereham to Wymondham, in open agricultural country with many woods and trees in the vicinity. The widely scattered village is very attractive with its well-tended gardens bright with flowers, and its lovely church.

The sign was designed by a local man, Mr. Jim Houston, and made by a Norfolk craftsman who prefers to remain anonymous. It is gratifying to the observer to look at a sign and to be able to interpret it without any prompting. It shows that it was erected to celebrate the Silver Jubilee, and is also surmounted by a crown. Within a circle an agricultural scene is depicted, showing a wood in the background, and a windmill and a plough in action in the foreground. This, of course implies that farming is the main industry, as the large fields of varied crops noticeably testifies. In the village you will see the windmill still standing, and it would be here that the locally grown corn would have been ground. The name Wicklewood perhaps makes you think, as some do, that witches were to be found here; but our old and trusted friend "The Oxford Dictionary of English Place Names" gives it as its derivative "wych elm wood"; and further information as to the significance of wych elms can be found in Edward Step's book "Wayside and Woodland Trees" in which he opines that whereas wych hazel rods were used to detect water, wych elm rods — or branches — were used with which to detect witches! In the days when witches were dreaded and feared, the wych elms would surely have been valuable assets, and it would be most unlikely that witches would venture anywhere near them — rather the very reverse!

WICKLEWOOD

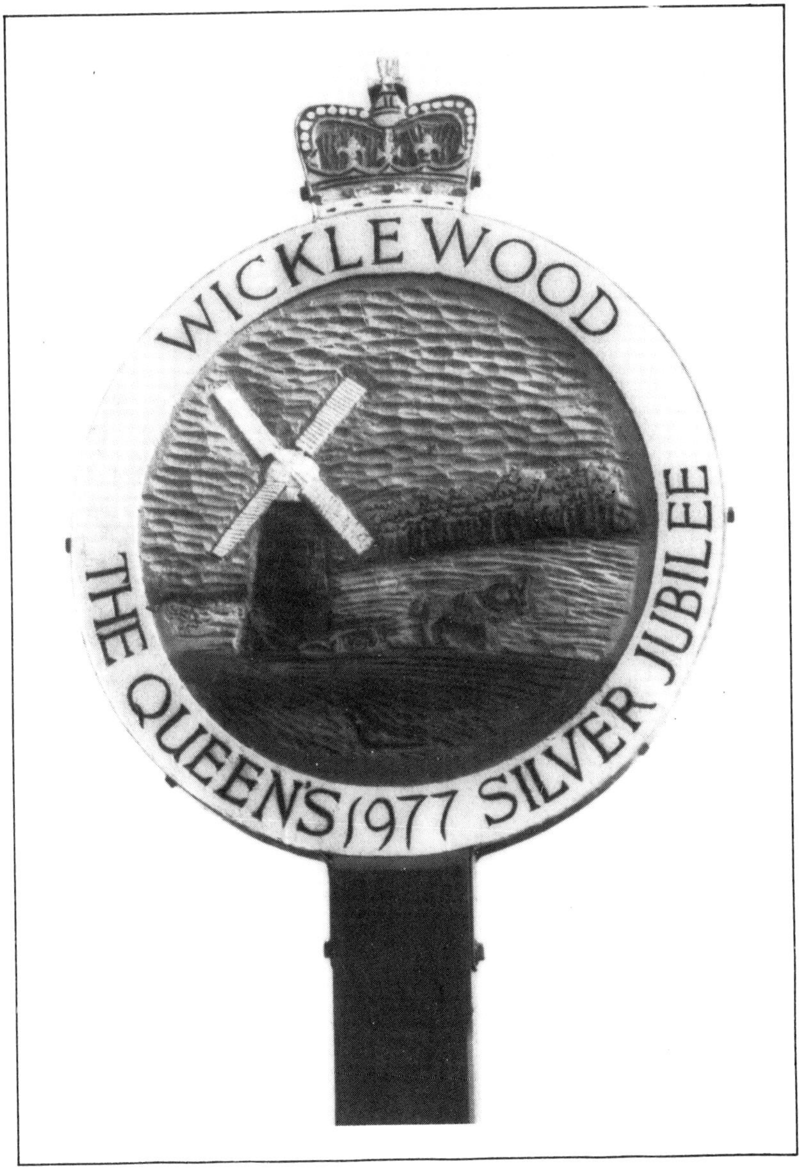
WICKLEWOOD
THE QUEEN'S 1977 SILVER JUBILEE

WIGGENHALL ST. MARY MAGDALEN

There are four Wiggenhalls, all near together, with a saint's name to distinguish them one from another. They are to be found in the fens, roughly between King's Lynn and Downham Market. They are all in the vicinity of the Great Ouse, and lie two on each side of the river. The country here is flat, but the soil is very fertile, and much of the agriculture here is similar to intensive market gardening.

The village sign at Wiggenhall St. Mary Magdalen shows a representation of the facade of a religious house with two figures, wearing a religious habit of no specific order, standing outside a large central archway. There were originally two religious houses, in no way connected, lying two miles apart, and not necessarily concurrently, and both it is believed, for nuns. It is not known what either of them looked like, for it was all so long ago, but in this sign the one building represents them both, and the two figures represent one from each foundation. The situation of one is unknown, but it is reasonable to assume that it might have been on the site of the 17th century Priory cottages, east of the church. But the other was known as Crabhouse Nunnery, and it was situated about two miles south of the church, on a bank of the river, and is marked on the map. It was founded in 1181 by Roger the Priest, the Prior of Normansburgh in South Rainham, and granted to Lena, a nun, daughter of Godric de Lynn. It was for the use of a prioress and seven nuns of the Augustinian order. The private house built on the same site is called Crabbs Abbey Farm.

The sign was made by Mr. Harry Carter, and stands near the church.

Near WIGGENHALL ST MARY MAGDALEN

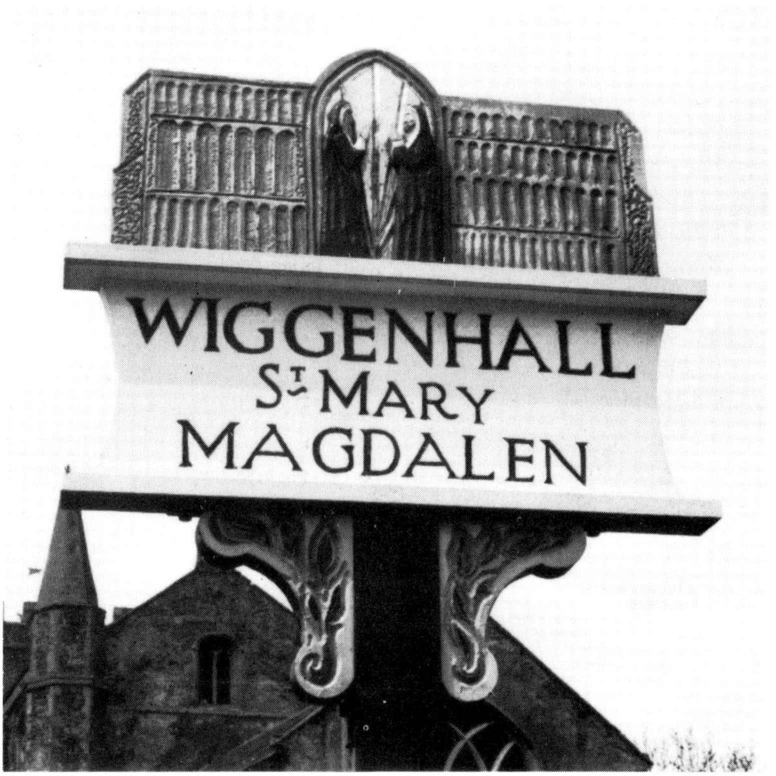
WIGGENHALL
S^T MARY
MAGDALEN

WINFARTHING

Winfarthing is one of those delightful Norfolk villages which seem to have grown as naturally out of the ground as the many lovely trees and copses which belong to the natural landscape of which they are all a part. Its varied houses, with roofs of pantiles or thatch, in their pleasant gardens look homely and inviting. Wherever one looks in the neighbourhood one can discern that farming is the way of life here, as it is in most of the county.

The village sign is colourful and looks interesting, and has a different theme from any that we have seen so far. The motif which surmounts the central panel shows a man driving a plough drawn by two horses which, by now, needs no explanation! On the big panel one sees, in front of the church, part of a large oak tree and beneath it stands a deer. You are now in the heart of what was once an extensive deer forest of 1,000 acres, reserved exclusively for hunting. It belonged originally to the Earl of Arundel, later passing to the Duke of Albemarle. The small medallion shaped panel on the left of the sign bears the betters E R I, and is a reminder that Queen Elizabeth I granted to the men of Winfarthing exemption from the duty of sitting on a jury so that they could continue to guard the estate from poachers and marauders. The oak itself is of great significance, for it was one of the largest in all England. Even when Domesday Book was written it was already 100 years old. It grew to such a great size that it had a girth of 70 feet. In all it had a life span of 1600 years, until it was ultimately destroyed in a fierce gale in 1947. Also to be seen on the panel are some village stocks, and seven loaves of bread, a record of the Easter bread which was a charity gift to the poor of the parish. Finally there is the large sword carved down the middle of the post. This was known as "The Good Sword of Winfarthing"; and the story goes that it was left behind in the churchyard by a criminal seeking sanctury in the church. It became an object of great superstition, and was enshrined by the monks in the church, for it had gained the reputation for being able to help people to find their stolen goods, and for helping women to lose unwanted husbands! It disappeared eventually when many abuses and superstitious practices were abolished.

WINFARTHING

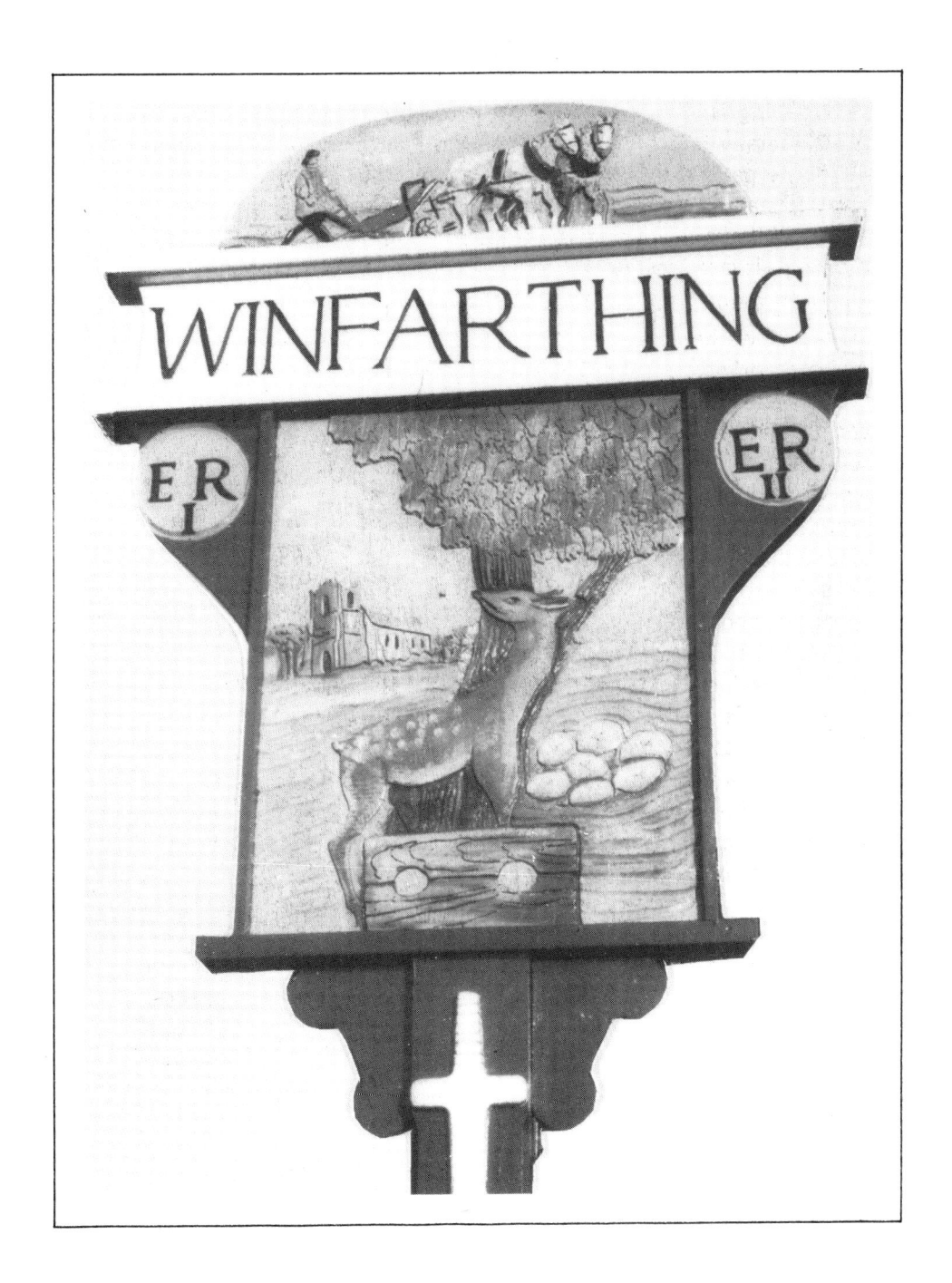

The small panel on the right bears the symbol E R II, signifying that the sign was erected to commemorate the Silver Jubilee of Queen Elizabeth II. The cost of the sign was paid for by the parishioners of Winfarthing; and the young people of the parish generously and thoughtfully presented the teak seat alongside it. The sign was made by Mr. Harry Carter of Swaffham, and the stone base by Mr. Alfred Stratton.

WRENINGHAM

Great originality has been shown at Wreningham, in this village sign, both in subject matter and workmanship; so that it ranks amongst the most attractive in the county. The first syllable of the name brings to mind the wren, that dainty little bird which we delight to see in our gardens, with its tiny mossed-lined nest, containing many small eggs. If we do not see it, we may hear its loud, clear voice trilling at all seasons of the year. This exquisite little bird is the theme of the sign, which is made of natural polished oak; it is T-shaped, and backed by a large circle on which is carved "All Saints St. Mary St. Stephen" the names of the former parishes which ultimately formed the present parish of Wreningham. Recessed in the panel running down the post of the sign is an intricately cut carving illustrating a story of witchcraft in days when witches were believed in, and were feared and shunned. Beneath this panel is yet another panel which in clear lettering gives an interpretation of the picture above it, which runs thus:- "A C13 century lady of the manor was a witch dominating it to evil purpose. A knight failed to kill her because she changed into a wren. She comes back every St. Stephen's day and is hunted by the villagers who beat the hedges with sticks and carry the dead wren in triumph". How terrifying for this innocent little bird to be the victim of this cruel and superstitious practice.

This legend is not pecular to Norfolk. and is heard of in other places also.

WRENINGHAM

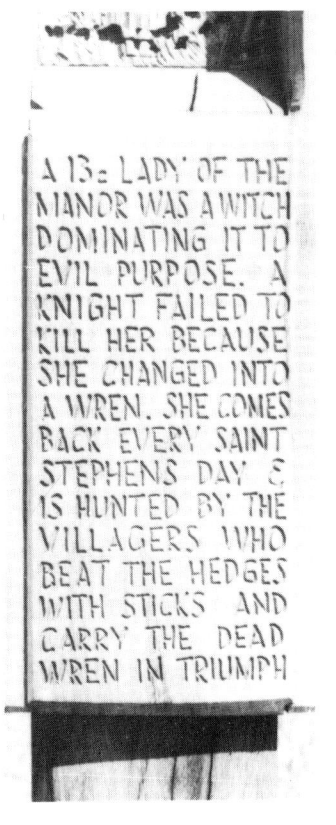

Do not miss seeing this fine sign if it is possible. It is certainly unlike any other of the signs we have seen so far, and it was created by local talent. It was designed by an architect, Mr. John Farrant, and the excellent carving was carried out by Mr. Ian Foster. It stands on a suitably made base, in the centre of the village, on a small triangular green.

YAXHAM

Yaxham is quite a busy thoroughfare, some two miles south of East Dereham, but the Church of St. Peter stands at the head of a quiet little lane leading from the road junction where the Village Sign is situated.

The money for a Village Sign is usually raised by groups of people working to that end, or by societies such as the Women's Institute, but this one was presented by a Mr. Temple, who with his wife came to live in Yaxham and spent a while there in happy retirement. Sadly, before long Mrs. Temple died, but not before they had both been impressed by their friendly reception by the Yaxham people. This fact is recorded on the brass plaque on the base of the sign, "Presented to friendly Yaxham in memory of Sheila Temple 1973."

On the Sign itself we see a carving of St. Peter's Church, and beside it a poet with a scroll in his hand. On the post, beneath the name, is a sundial to remind us of the one on the church itself.

The Reverend John Johnson was rector of Yaxham for 36 years, and it was he who brought his famous kinsman, the poet William Cowper, back to Norfolk for the last few years of the poet's life, and it was at Johnson's house in East Dereham that Cowper died in 1800.

It is interesting to note that the two succeeding rectors of Yaxham bore the name of William Cowper Johnson.

Mr. Harry Carter made the sign and the flints incorporated in the base were collected by the local schoolchildren.

YAXHAM

YAXHAM

VILLAGE AND TOWN SIGNS IN NORFOLK

1 Acle
2 Aldborough
3 Antingham
4 Attleborough
5 Bacton
6 Banham
7 Bawburgh
8 Beeston
9 Belton
10 Bodham
11 Bradwell
12 Bressingham
13 Briston
14 Brundall
15 Burgh Castle
16 Burnham Thorpe
17 Buxton
18 Cantley
19 Carbrooke
20 Corpusty & Saxthorpe
21 Crimplesham
22 Gt. Dunham
23 Edingthorpe
24 Felthorpe
25 Filby
26 Framingham Earl
27 Happisburgh
28 Hempnall
29 Hempton Green
30 Hethersett
31 Hevingham
32 Hickling
33 Hockwold-cum-Wilton
34 Holt
35 Horsford
36 Horsham St. Faith
37 Hunstanton (Old)
38 East Lexham
39 West Lexham
40 West Lynn
41 Marham
42 Martham
43 Melton Constable
44 Mileham
45 Mundesley
46 Mundford
47 Neatishead
48 Outwell
49 Overstrand
50 Palling (or Sea Palling)
51 Paston
52 Pentney
53 Potter Heigham
54 Pulham St. Mary
55 Quidenham
56 Raveningham
57 Repps (North)
58 Rollesby
59 Roydon
60 Rudham (East)
61 Runton (West)
62 Rushall
63 Gt. Ryburgh
64 Scole
65 Scottow
66 Sheringham
67 Shotesham
68 Gt. Snoring
69 Southery
70 Spixworth
71 Sporle
72 Stanhoe
73 Stibbard
74 Stiffkey
75 Stoke Ferry
76 Sutton
77 Swainsthorpe
78 Terrington St. Clement
79 Terrington St. John
80 Thorpe End
81 Thorpe Market
82 Three Holes
83 Thurton
84 Thwaite St. Mary
85 Tilney All Saints
86 Tilney St. Lawrence
87 Tittleshall
88 Trunch
89 Upton with Fishley
90 Walsham (South)
91 Gt. Walsingham
92 Watlington
93 Welney
94 Wereham
95 Weston Longville
96 Wicklewood
97 Wiggenhall St. Mary Magdalen
98 Winfarthing
99 Wreningham
100 Yaxham

BLACK HORSE BOOKS

8 & 10 WENSUM STREET
NORWICH, NR3 1HR

THE STORY OF ELY & ITS CATHEDRAL
   By Bernard E. Dorman First published 1945
   Seventh revised and enlarged edition.
   98 + x pages. 23 illustrations, 3 plans
                Cloth bound edition £8.95
                Paperback   £4.95

VILLAGE SIGNS IN NORFOLK
   By Frances Procter & Philippa Miller
   First published 1973. New edition
                Book 1 Paperback £5.95
                Book 2 Paperback £5.95
                Book 3 Paperback £5.95
                Book 4 In preparation

Printed by Crowes of Norwich, 11 Concorde Road, Norwich NR6 6BJ. Telephone: (0603) 403349.